World Geography

PRACTICE FOR THE TEXAS ASSESSMENT

MASTER THE TEKS

networks™
A Social Studies Learning System

McGraw Hill Education

Bothell, WA • Chicago, IL • Columbus, OH • New York, NY

mheonline.com

McGraw Hill Education

Send all inquiries to:
McGraw-Hill Education
8787 Orion Place
Columbus, OH 43240

ISBN: 978-0-02-141594-6
MHID: 0-02-141594-3

Printed in the United States of America.

2 3 4 5 6 7 RHR 20 19 18 17 16 15

Introduction

History

Geography

Economics

Government

Citizenship

Culture

Science, Technology, and Society

World Geography Assessment Practice Test

What's in this book and how do I use it?

There are two distinct sections in this workbook:

- **TEKS Practice Questions**

  For each TEKS, you'll find a set of practice questions. The practice questions are either multiple-choice questions or griddable questions designed to assess your understanding of the materials covered in the TEKS.

  After you answer each set of practice questions, check your answers to assess how well you understand the material. This will help you determine if you need to review the content covered by this TEKS.

- **World Geography Assessment Practice Test**

  After the practice questions, you'll find a 68-question practice test. This test will assess TEKS covered in the World Geography assessment test.

Name ______________________ Date ______________ Class __________

TEKS 1A

Choose the best answer for each question. Circle the letter for the correct answer, or record your answer and fill in the bubbles on the provided griddable.

1 This map shows the five world culture hearths.

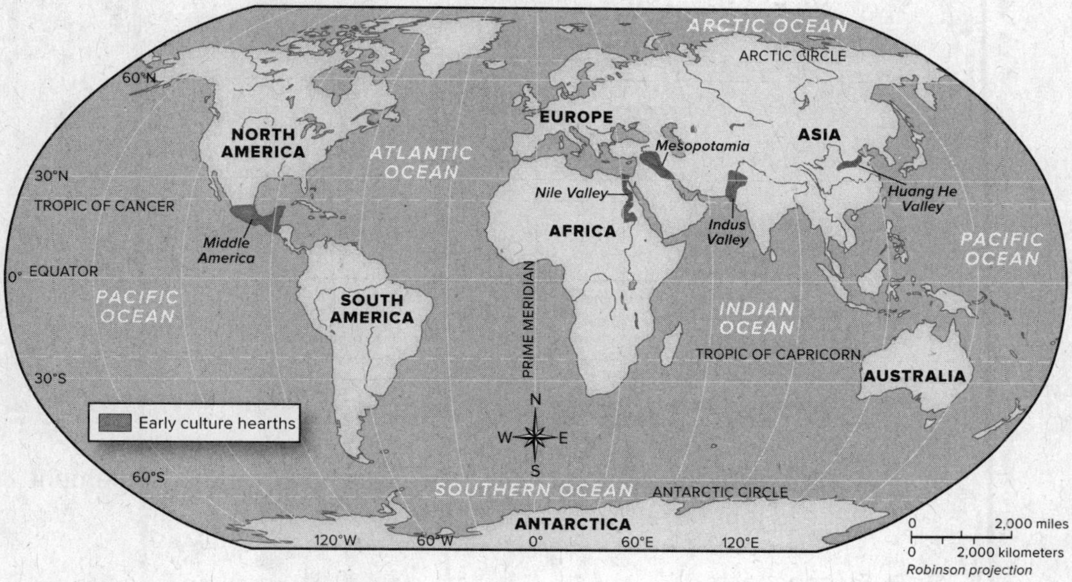

The culture regions have common geographic features, including

A fertile land and a mild climate.

B a location on a seacoast.

C mountains.

D earthquakes.

Name ______________________ Date ______________ Class ________

History

TEKS 1A

2 This map shows the European settlement of Australia.

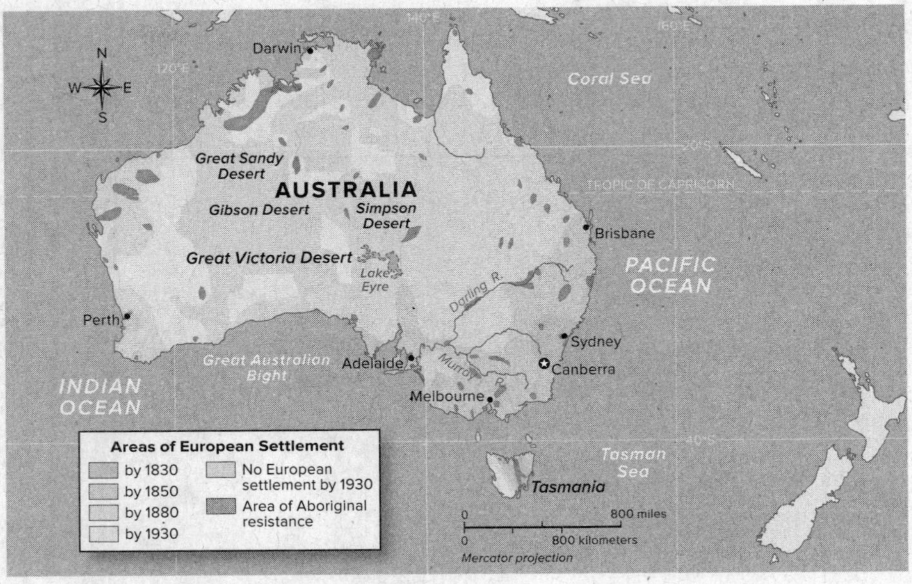

According to the map, by 1930, there was no European settlement in areas that were

F seacoasts.

G mountains.

H far north.

J deserts.

---

3 The first settlers in the Texas Hill Country came mainly from Tennessee (Appalachian Mountains) and Missouri and Arkansas (Ozark and Ouachita Mountains). Which statement best describes what they found attractive in the Hill Country as their new home?

A It had a lot of factories, where the migrants could find jobs.

B It had the same forests as they had known in their former homes.

C There were many slaves in the Hill Country to do farmwork.

D The hills reminded them of the mountains in their former home.

Check your answers.
If you missed 0, great job!
If you missed 1, not bad.
If you missed 2-3, review the effects of physical and human geographic patterns on the past.

Name ______________________ Date ______________ Class ________

History

TEKS 1B

Choose the best answer for each question. Circle the letter for the correct answer, or record your answer and fill in the bubbles on the provided griddable.

1 Pizza is made of ingredients that were part of the Columbian Exchange. Wheat (for the crust) was taken from Europe to the Americas, and tomatoes and peppers were taken from the Americas to Europe. The Columbian Exchange is an example of

A cultural diffusion.

B migration.

C a trade treaty.

D agriculture.

---

2 The predominant religion in Latin America today is Catholicism because

F the Catholic Church was founded in Mexico.

G Spanish missionaries who came with the conquerors converted the indigenous peoples.

H traditional religions blended together through a process of syncretism.

J indigenous peoples had no religious beliefs at all until the Spanish came.

History

TEKS 1B

3 "In the capital city of Nairobi, [Kenya,] nightclubs, movie theaters, and water parks are the norm. A very different lifestyle is found in rural communities, where 77 percent of Kenyans live."

Nightclubs, movie theaters, and water parks are part of modern Western culture. Such features tend to diffuse

A from countryside to city.

B by government directive.

C in certain climate zones.

D to cities first, then to the countryside.

Check your answers.
If you missed 0, great job!
If you missed 1, not bad.
If you missed 2-3, review how processes of diffusion influenced events in the past and helped shape the present.

Name ______________________ Date ______________ Class ________

History

TEKS 2A

Choose the best answer for each question. Circle the letter for the correct answer, or record your answer and fill in the bubbles on the provided griddable.

1 This table compares some characteristics of Mexico under Spanish colonial rule and after independence.

Under Spanish Colonial Rule	After Independence
Ruled by all-powerful viceroys	Ruled by military dictators called caudillos
Social hierarchy with landowners, Catholic clergy, and army officers the most powerful	Social hierarchy with landowners, Catholic clergy, and army officers most powerful
No democracy	Occasional moves toward democracy

Three centuries of Spanish rule continued to be an influence in Mexico after independence in that

A there was widespread democracy.

B the Spanish army continued to occupy the country.

C power was concentrated in a small group of wealthy people.

D new agricultural crops were introduced.

---

2 In the late 1800s, Japan began to develop a modern economy and society under the Meiji Restoration. This helped to lay the groundwork for

F Japan's traditional culture.

G Japan's rapid recovery after World War II, to become the third-largest economy in the world.

H rugged topography and many earthquakes in Japan.

J the Japanese language.

Name ______________________ Date ______________ Class ________

History

TEKS 2A

3 A World Wildlife Fund reported what was happening to Lebanon's famous forests.

> ***"Most forest fires in Lebanon start when a fire set by a farmer to clear his orchards and fields of grasses and stubble gets out of control. The problem has become worse over the last decade because of changing land use.***
>
> ***In the past, villagers used scrubby bushes from the forests as fuel for cooking, which kept the dry undergrowth thin. Now there's electricity, so the undergrowth stays thick—perfect fuel for fires."***
>
> **—World Wildlife Fund, "Lebanon's Forests: Facing New Threats"**

According to the report, the major cause of loss of forests in Lebanon is

A climate change.

B logging of valuable timber.

C erosion.

D wildfires.

Check your answers.
If you missed 0, great job!
If you missed 1, not bad.
If you missed 2-3, review how past events are related to current characteristics

Name ______________________ Date ______________ Class ________

History

TEKS 2B

Choose the best answer for each question. Circle the letter for the correct answer, or record your answer and fill in the bubbles on the provided griddable.

1 Which of these uses of the Chang Jiang (Yangtze) River in China represents a recent change in the Chinese economy and society?

A water for irrigating rice crops

B transportation

C water for drinking and household use

D hydroelectricity

---

2 The Aborigines of Australia were nomadic hunters and gatherers. European settlers sought land for farming and livestock ranching as well as mineral resources. Therefore, land use in the Outback (the vast interior plateau) of Australia reflected this change in that

F groups of families owned and farmed land communally.

G land was claimed by individuals as private property.

H large cities grew up in the Outback.

J small groups of related people moved around, seeking food and water.

TEKS 2B

3 Daniel Boone led early settlers into eastern Kentucky in the late 1700s. They established small farms in the mountain valleys and cut timber from the mountains for building and for fuel. With the Industrial Revolution, what was a new use for the mountains?

A large-scale farms to grow food for the rapidly growing cities

B ski resorts for recreation for urban people

C coal for eastern industries

D gold

Check your answers.
If you missed 0, great job!
If you missed 1, not bad.
If you missed 2-3, review how changes in society lead to changes in the use of physical features

Name ______________________ Date ______________ Class __________

TEKS 3A

Choose the best answer for each question. Circle the letter for the correct answer, or record your answer and fill in the bubbles on the provided griddable.

1 Scientists have been keeping records of temperatures in Dallas, Texas, for more than 100 years.

Average Monthly Temperatures for Dallas, Texas (° F.)		
Year	**January**	**July**
1900	47.3	80.7
1910	48.2	85.0
1920	43.0	82.8
1930	35.2	86.5
1940	34.9	81.6
1950	47.9	81.3
1960	44.1	84.6
1970	40.6	84.0
1980	45.5	92.0
1990	51.8	82.5
2000	50.6	87.3
2010	44.3	85.9

Source: National Weather Service Weather Forecast Office, www.srh.noaa.gov/fwd/?n=dmotemp

The data shown support which of these statements?

A The Northern Hemisphere receives more energy from the sun in January than in July.

B The Northern Hemisphere receives more energy from the sun in July than in January.

C The Northern Hemisphere receives the same amount of energy from the sun all year.

D The data tell us nothing about the amount of energy received from the sun.

TEKS 3A

2 The table below shows the average length of daylight in Houston, Texas, for each month of the year.

Month	Average Hours and Minutes of Daylight
January	10:25
February	11:04
March	11:55
April	12:51
May	13:37
June	14:01
July	13:50
August	13:10
September	12:17
October	11:22
November	10:36
December	10:13

The month when the Northern Hemisphere is pointed toward the sun is

F March.

G September.

H December.

J June.

Name ______________________ Date ______________ Class __________

TEKS 3A

3 John and Molly moved from the United States to New Zealand in January. Which statement best describes what they experienced?

A They went from summer in the United States to summer in New Zealand.

B They went from winter in the United States t winter in New Zealand.

C They went from winter in the United States to summer in New Zealand.

D They went from summer in the United States to winter in New Zealand.

Check your answers.
If you missed 0, great job!
If you missed 1, not bad.
If you missed 2-3, review how weather and climate are related to annual changes in Earth-sun relationships.

Name ______________________ Date ______________ Class __________

TEKS 3B

Geography

1 Richard Stone wrote an article for a magazine about the effects of a meteorite hitting Earth.

> ***"The heat incinerated herds of reindeer and charred tens of thousands of evergreens across hundreds of square miles. For days, and for thousands of miles around, the sky remained bright with an eerie orange glow—as far away as western Europe people were able to read newspapers at night without a lamp."***
>
> **—Richard Stone, "The Last Great Impact on Earth,"**
> ***Discover,* September 1996**

Which statement describes this effect?

A Wildlife in the region ran away.

B The environment froze into a huge ice cap.

C The hot meteorite started a massive forest fire.

D The meteorite created a large crater.

---

2 The Ring of Fire is an earthquake-prone zone that surrounds the

F the Pacific Ocean.

G the Atlantic Ocean.

H North America.

J the Caribbean Sea.

Name ______________________ Date ______________ Class __________

TEKS 3B

3 This diagram shows the forces at work in plate tectonics.

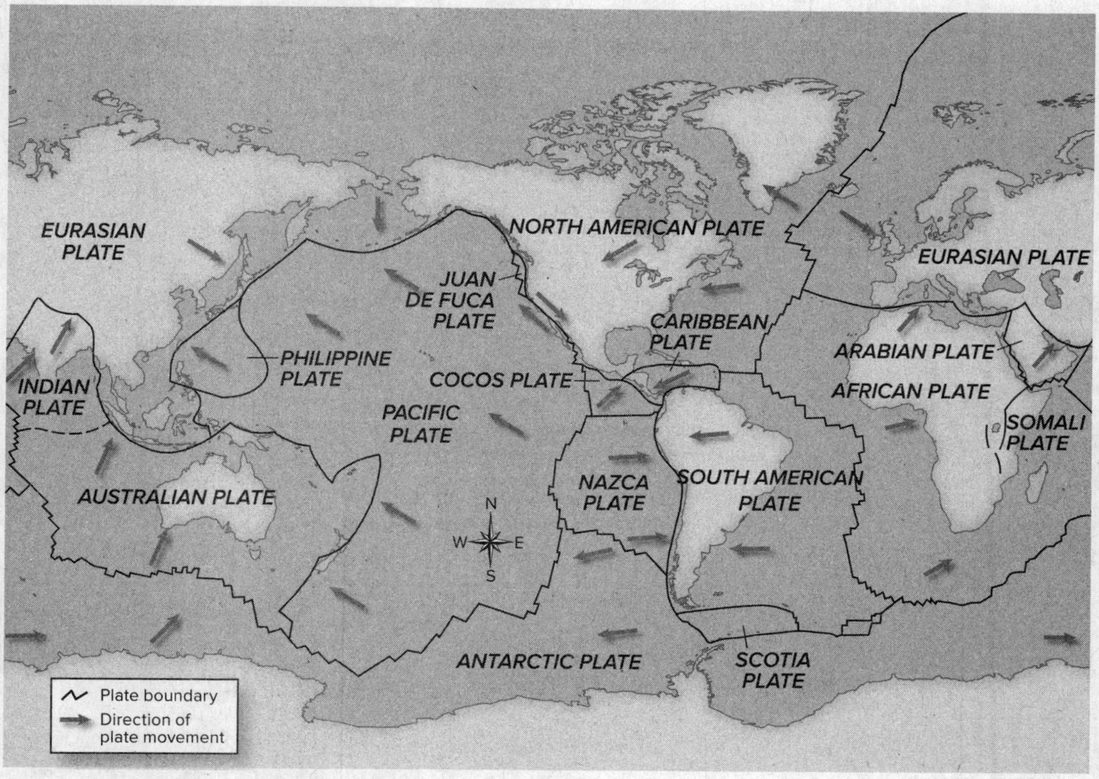

According to the diagram, the movement of which plates formed the Andes?

A Nazca and South American

B Arabian and Eurasian

C Indian and Eurasian

D Juan de Fuca and North American

Check your answers.
If you missed 0, great job!
If you missed 1, not bad.
If you missed 2-3, review how physical processes shape patterns in the physical environment.

Name ______________________ Date ______________ Class __________

TEKS 3C

Choose the best answer for each question. Circle the letter for the correct answer, or record your answer and fill in the bubbles on the provided griddable.

1 Water moves through a cycle, changing from one form to another.

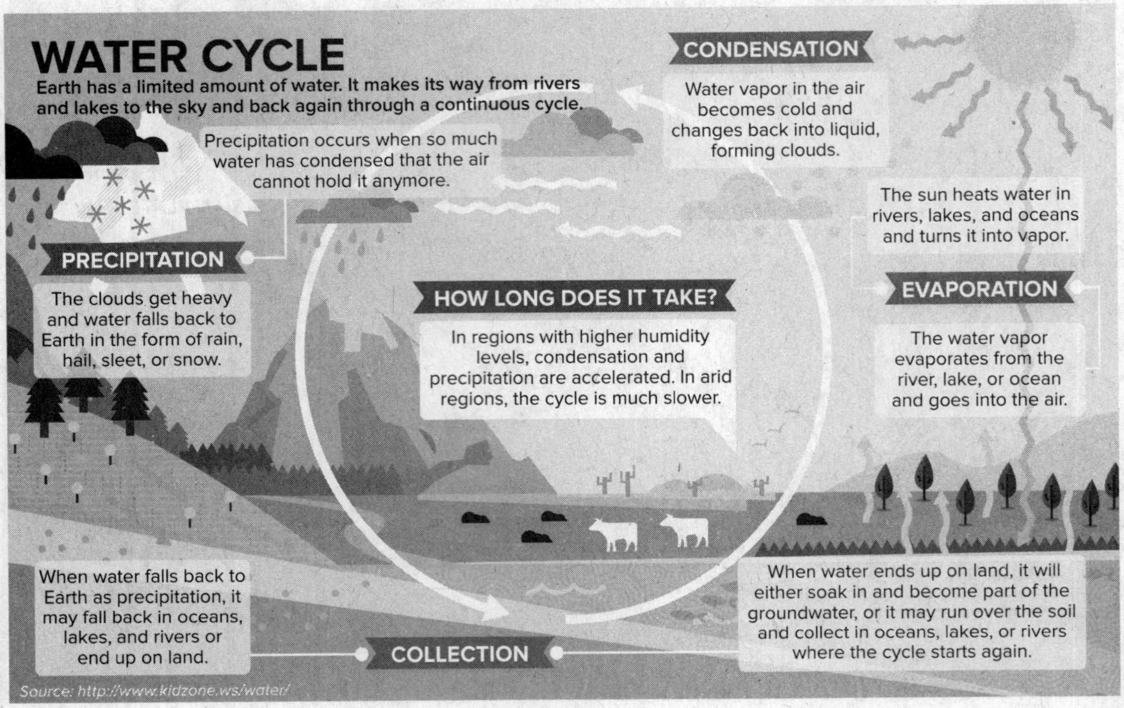

According to the diagram, the process of changing from liquid water to water vapor is

A precipitation.

B evaporation.

C condensation.

D collection.

---

2 People can live on the international space station because

F they have brought a piece of Earth with them.

G mechanical systems provide life support.

H they stay for only brief periods.

J outer space is just like Earth's surface.

Name ______ Date ______ Class ______

TEKS 3C

3 The gas that makes up the largest portion of the atmosphere is

A hydrogen.

B oxygen.

C carbon dioxide.

D nitrogen.

Geography

Check your answers.
If you missed 0, great job!
If you missed 1, not bad.
If you missed 2-3, review physical processes that affect the lithosphere, atmosphere, hydrosphere, and biosphere.

Name ______________________ Date ______________ Class __________

TEKS 4A

Choose the best answer for each question. Circle the letter for the correct answer, or record your answer and fill in the bubbles on the provided griddable.

1 India receives almost all its rainfall in summer.

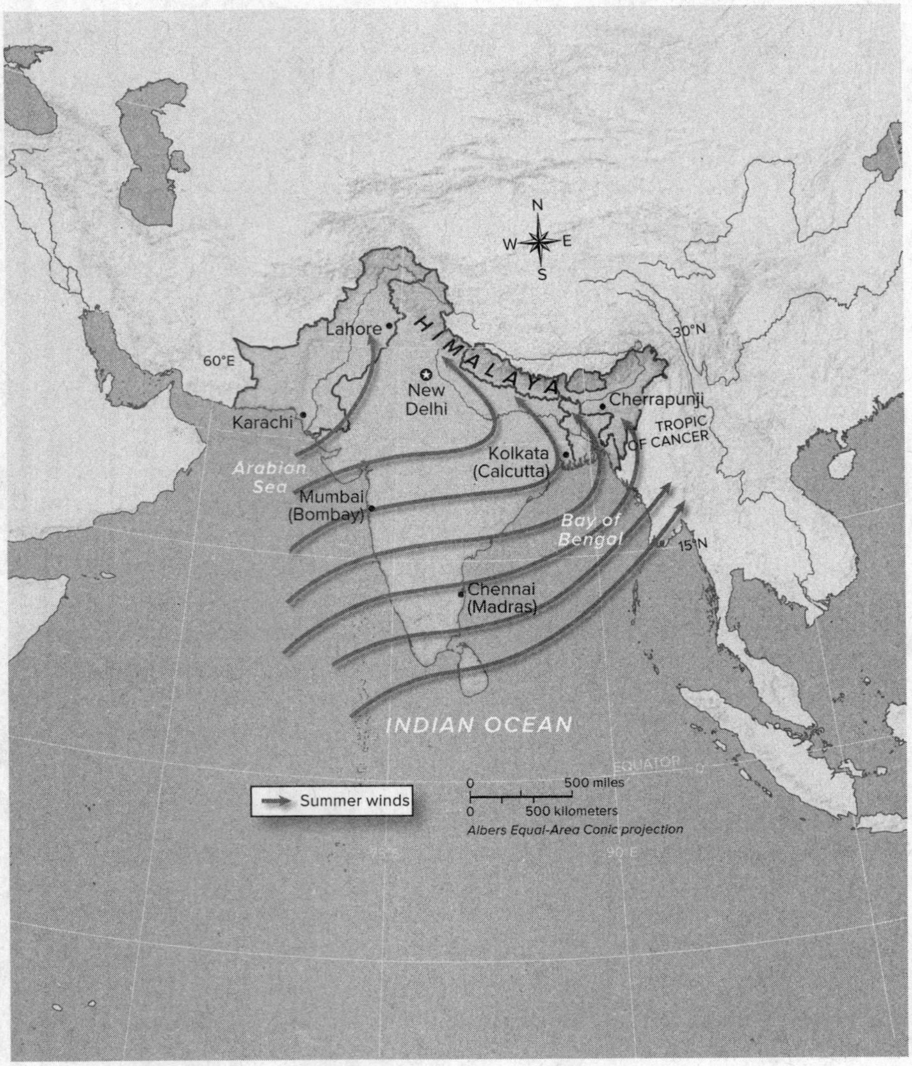

Why do the winds turn west over the Gangetic Plain rather than continuing to the north?

A The rotation of Earth on its axis steers them.

B The Himalaya Mountains form a barrier that blocks the winds.

C People built a dam in order to increase rainfall.

D The map is inaccurate—the winds do continue to flow northward.

TEKS 4A

2 In China, more precipitation falls in the south and east than in the north and west.

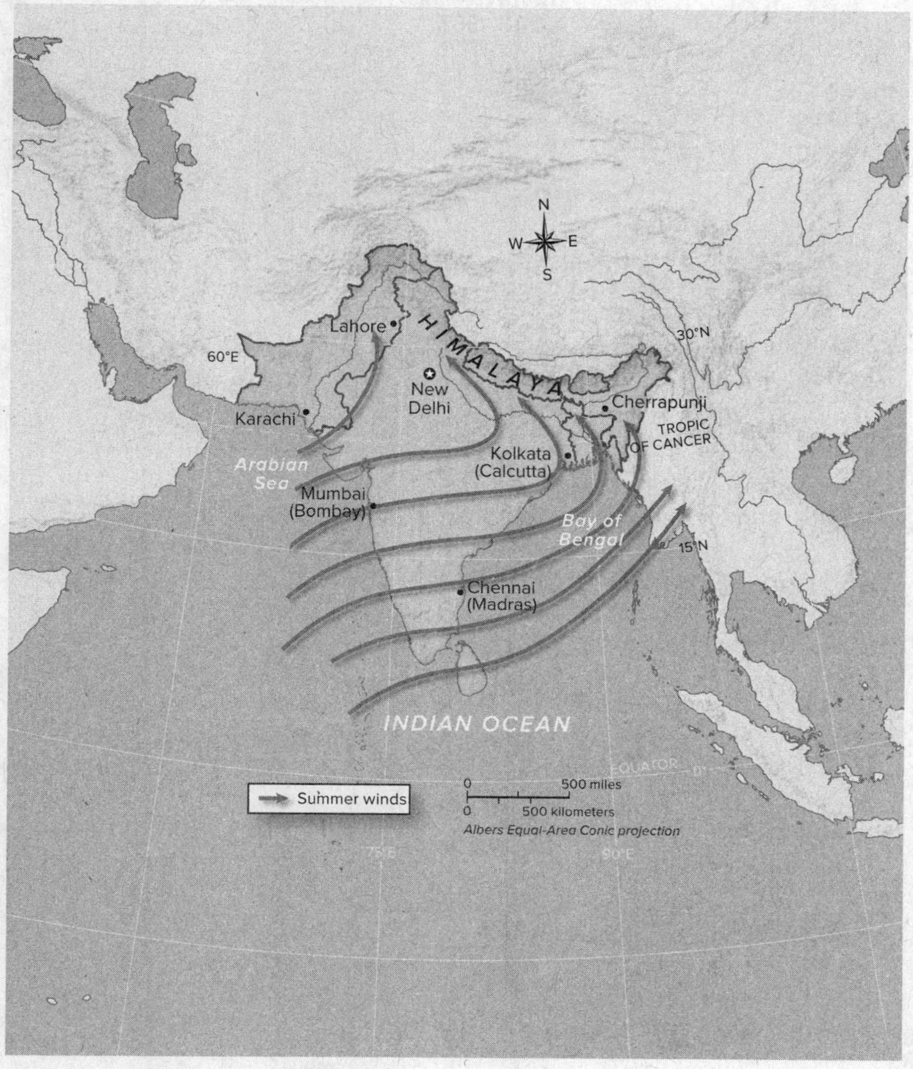

Why is much of northwestern China desert?

F A high-pressure area blocks the southern winds.

G Much of the moisture in the winds off the ocean falls on the mountains and hills of southern China, so that the air that reaches the northwest is dry.

H The Great Wall of China blocks the rain-bearing winds.

J Crops in southeastern China promote precipitation, but crops in the northwest do not.

Name ______________________ Date ______________ Class ____________

TEKS 4A

3 Temperature changes with elevation above sea level.

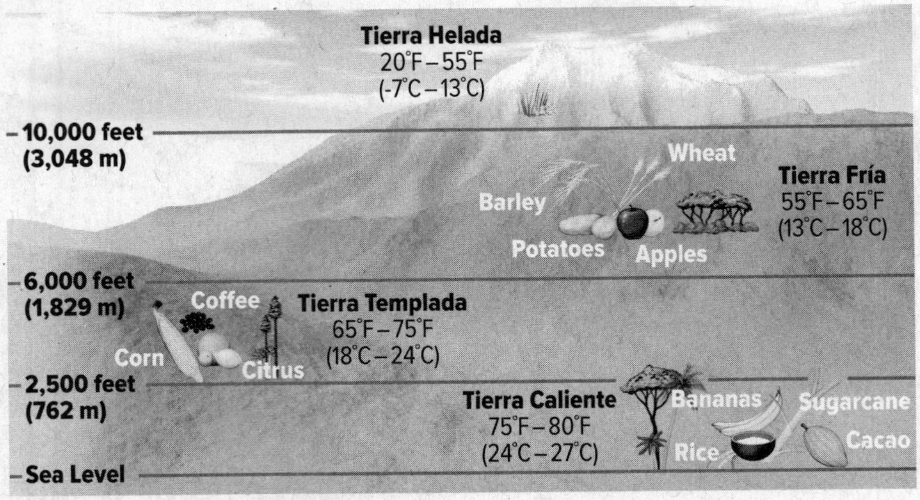

Temperatures below freezing are found above

A 2,000 feet (610 m).

B 5,000 feet (1,524 m).

C 7,500 feet (2,286 m).

D 10,000 feet (3,048 m).

Check your answers.
If you missed 0, great job!
If you missed 1, not bad.
If you missed 2-3, review how elevation, latitude, wind systems, ocean currents, position on a continent, and mountain barriers influence climate.

Name ______________________ Date ______________ Class __________

TEKS 4B

Choose the best answer for each question. Circle the letter for the correct answer, or record your answer and fill in the bubbles on the provided griddable.

1 The numerous north-south mountain ranges in mainland Southeast Asia were formed

A by volcanic eruptions in historic times.

B by the collision of the Indian and Eurasian tectonic plates.

C by accumulation of silt brought down by rivers.

D by action of ocean waves.

---

2 Atolls are created through a long process.

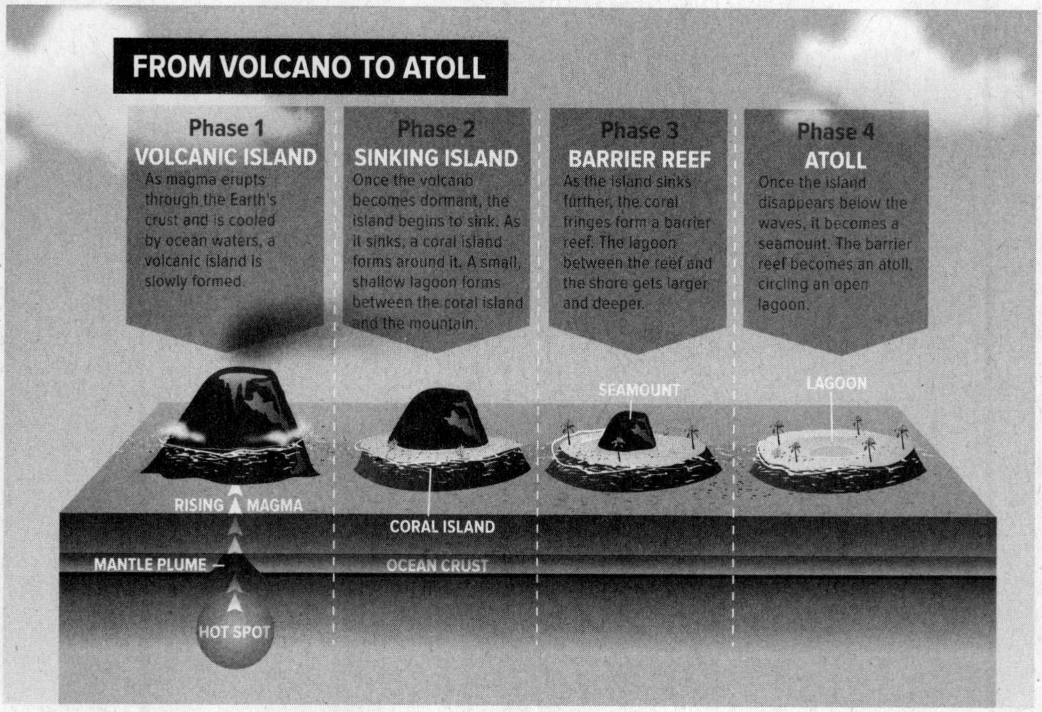

The ring of islands or islets that results is composed of

F volcanic rock.

G granite.

H coral.

J sedimentary rock.

Name ______________________ Date ______________ Class ________

TEKS 4B

3 Mountains may be built by folding and faulting of Earth's crust.

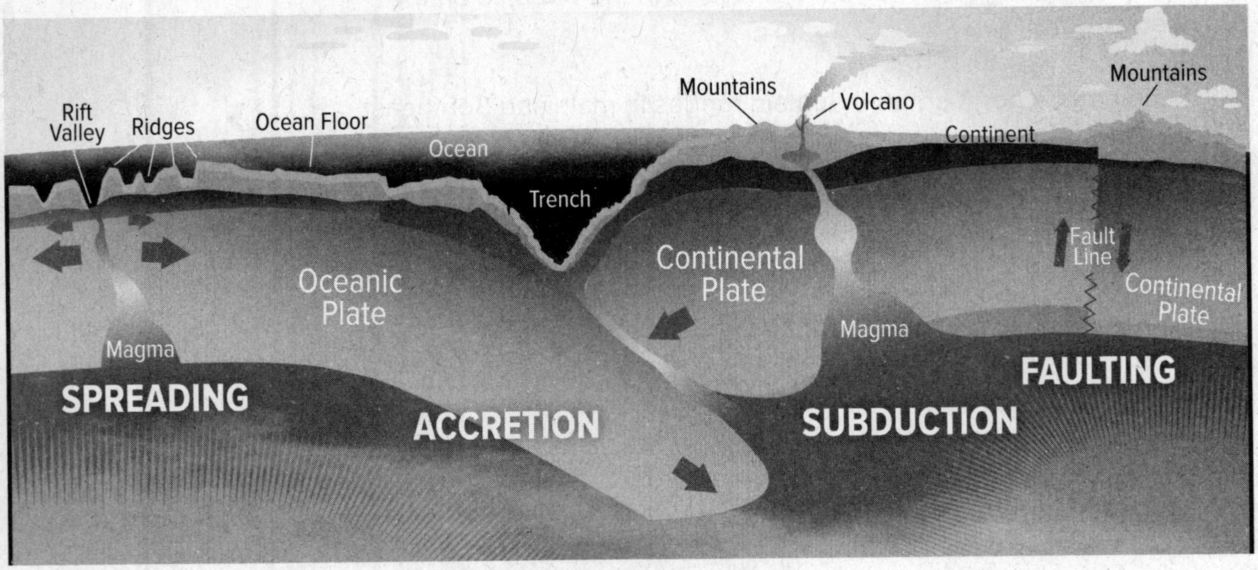

Faults occur when

A a meteorite strikes Earth and cracks it open.

B magma reaches the surface of Earth.

C ocean waves wash over a tectonic plate.

D pressures of moving plates become too great and the plate cracks.

Check your answers.
If you missed 0, great job!
If you missed 1, not bad.
If you missed 2-3, review physical processes that case the development of different landforms.

Name ______________________ Date ______________ Class ____________

TEKS 4C

Choose the best answer for each question. Circle the letter for the correct answer, or record your answer and fill in the bubbles on the provided griddable.

1 In the low latitude areas of Australia's north is a zone of tropical savanna, which supports marsupials like kangaroos and wallabies. South of this zone lie vast areas of desert, where vegetation is sparse. The main climatic factor that causes the difference is

A the amount of rainfall.

B the seasonal timing of rainfall.

C the average annual temperature.

D the difference in temperature from summer to winter.

---

2 As wind blows over the Cascade Mountains in the Pacific Northwest, it first cools and then warms.

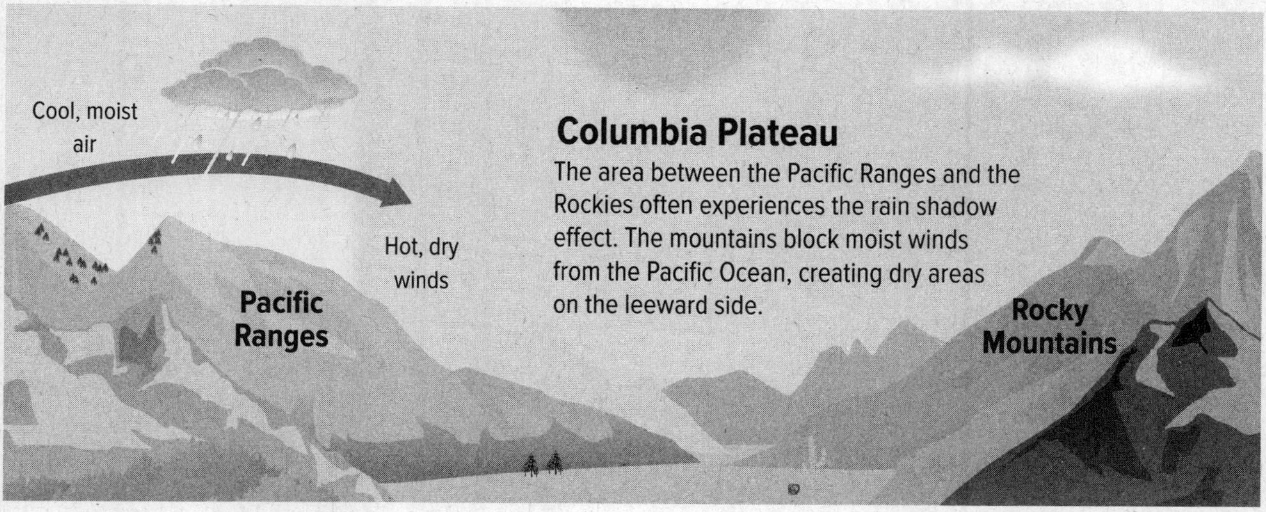

What kind of climate and biomes would you expect to find east of the Cascade Mountains?

F cool and rainy with dense forests

G warm and rainy with coniferous forests

H warm and dry with steppe vegetation

J cool and dry with desert

Name ______________________ Date ______________ Class __________

TEKS 4C

3 The major difference between the biomes supported by subarctic climates and the biomes in tundra climates is

A in subarctic climate areas, there are forests, while in tundra regions there are no trees.

B In tundra regions, there are no wild animals, while subarctic regions have animal life.

C tundra regions are warmer than subarctic regions and hence have more living species.

D tundra regions have more precipitation than subarctic regions, supporting more trees.

Geography

Check your answers.
If you missed 0, great job!
If you missed 1, not bad.
If you missed 2-3, review the influence of climate on the distribution of biomes in different regions.

Name ______________________ Date ______________ Class __________

TEKS 5A

Choose the best answer for each question. Circle the letter for the correct answer, or record your answer and fill in the bubbles on the provided griddable.

1 This table shows the percentages of population in Dallas and San Antonio who are of various races and are Hispanic and non-Hispanic.

	White	Black	Asian	Other	Two or more races	Hispanic	Non-Hispanic
Dallas	53.5	22.3	5.0	15.5	2.8	38.3	61.7
San Antonio	72.6	6.9	2.4	13.7	3.4	63.2	36.8

Source: U.S. Census Bureau

Compared with Dallas, San Antonio's character is probably

A less diverse.

B more influenced by Hispanic cultures.

C more influenced by Asian cultures.

D more similar to the classic "melting pot".

---

2 A Southeast Asian country that has an authoritarian government, has enacted strict rules (especially about cleanliness), enjoys an excellent seaport, and has become very wealthy is

F Myanmar (Burma).

G Vietnam.

H Singapore.

J Laos.

Name ______________________ Date ______________ Class __________

TEKS 5A

3 Makkah (Mecca) owes its importance to its role as a sacred city in the religion of

A Judaism.

B Christianity.

C Hinduism.

D Islam.

Geography

Check your answers.
If you missed 0, great job!
If you missed 1, not bad.
If you missed 2-3, review how character of a place is related to its political, economic, social, and cultural elements.

Name ______________________ Date ______________ Class ________

TEKS 5B

Choose the best answer for each question. Circle the letter for the correct answer, or record your answer and fill in the bubbles on the provided griddable.

1 The United Nations Development Programme's Human Development Index is calculated from indicators of a long and healthy life, knowledge, and a decent standard of living in a country. Some indicators for countries are:

Country	Life expectancy at birth	Mean years of schooling	Gross national income per capita (in $US)
A	66.5	10.4	19,441
B	75.3	7.5	11,477
C	82.5	12.8	41,524
D	63.1	4.9	1,636

Source: United Nations Human Development Programme, Human Development Reports

Which country has the highest Human Development Index?

A Country A

B Country B

C Country C

D Country D

---

2 This table shows the percentage of the workforce in various countries who work in different kinds of economic activities.

Country	Agriculture	Manufacturing	Services
A	2	18	79
B	39	13	48
C	13	24	62
D	30	17	53

Source: CIA World Factbook

Which of these countries is considered the least developed?

F Country A

G Country B

H Country C

J Country D

Geography

Name ______________________ Date ______________ Class ____________

TEKS 5B

3 This table shows the infant mortality rates for selected countries.

Country	Infant mortality per 1,000 live births
A	15.02
B	41.61
C	49.43
D	3.31

Source: CIA World Factbook

Which country probably has the highest female literacy rate?

A Country A

B Country B

C Country C

D Country D

Check your answers.
If you missed 0, great job!
If you missed 1, not bad.
If you missed 2-3, review political, economic, social, and demographic indicators.

Geography

Name ______________________ Date ______________ Class __________

TEKS 6A

Choose the best answer for each question. Circle the letter for the correct answer, or record your answer and fill in the bubbles on the provided griddable.

1 This map shows the average amount of precipitation per year in the Eastern Mediterranean.

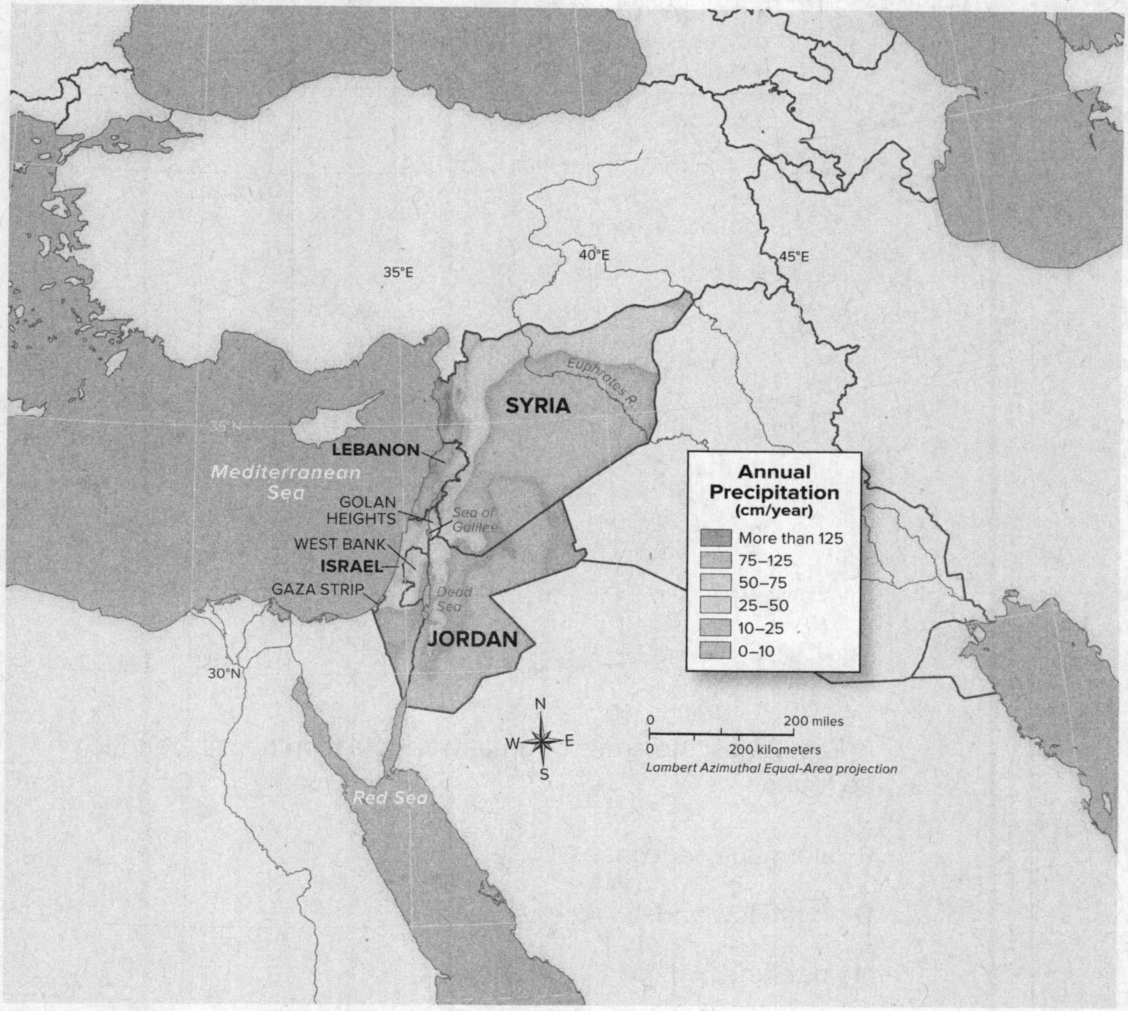

Which country would you expect to have the highest population density?

A Israel

B Lebanon

C Iraq

D Syria

Geography

TEKS 6A

2 This map shows the population density in East Africa.

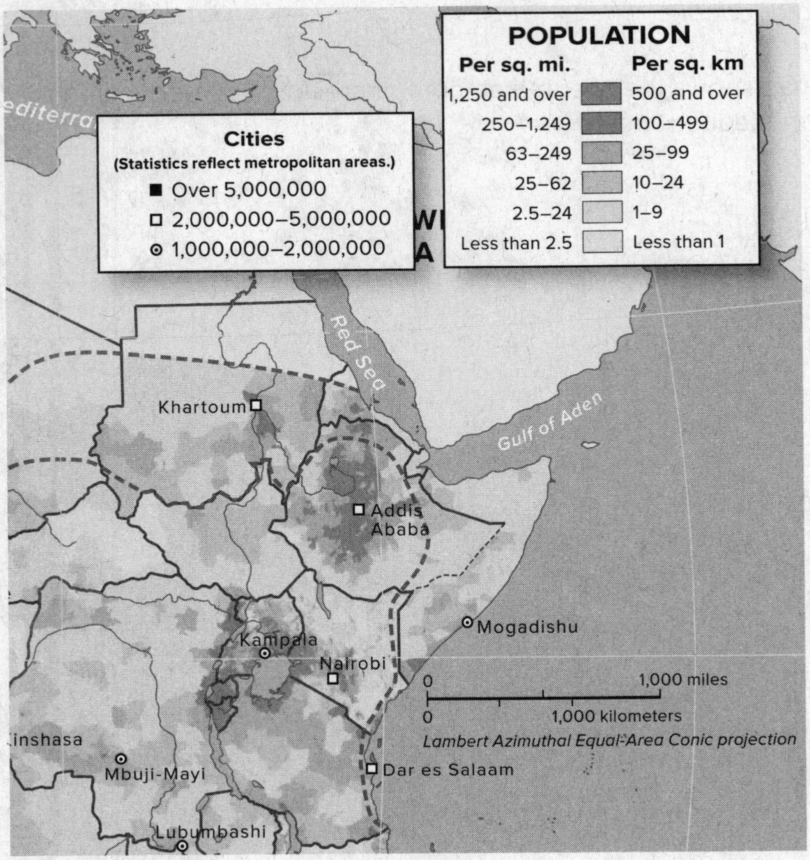

In East Africa, the areas of greatest population density tend to be found

F along the seacoast

G in the lowlands

H in the highlands

J along rivers

Name ______________________ Date ______________ Class ________

TEKS 6A

3 This map shows the population density of Egypt.

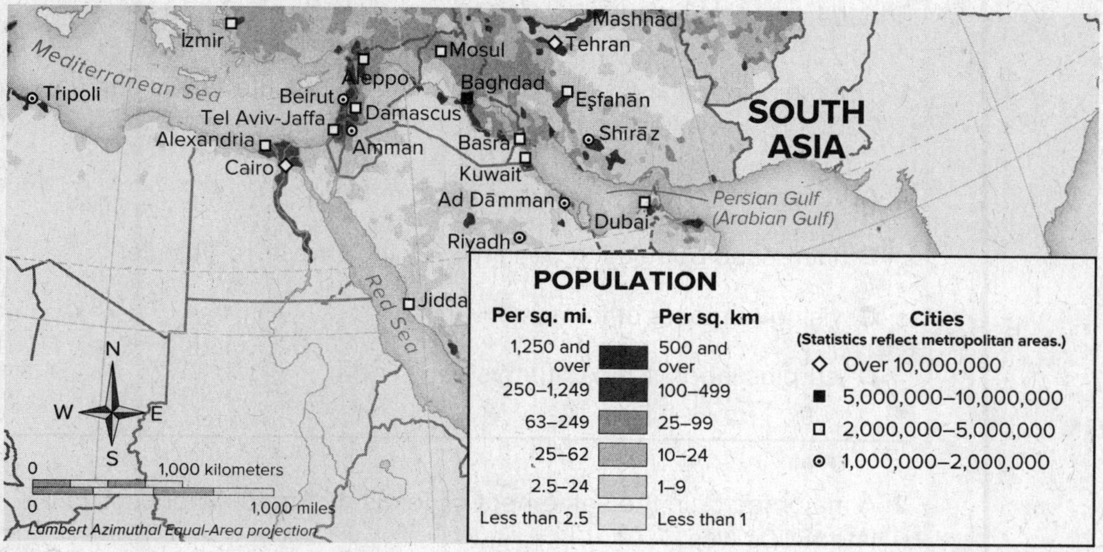

The area of greatest population density is

A along the Mediterranean Sea coast.

B along the Nile River.

C along the coast of the Red Sea.

D in the southwest.

Geography

Check your answers.
If you missed 0, great job!
If you missed 1, not bad.
If you missed 2-3, review the human and physical features that influence the size and distribution of settlements.

Name ______________________ Date ______________ Class __________

TEKS 6B

Choose the best answer for each question. Circle the letter for the correct answer, or record your answer and fill in the bubbles on the provided griddable.

1 The major population migration in China in the late 1900s and early 2000s has resulted in

A a majority of China's people living in cities.

B increased population density in China's western "frontier".

C rising numbers of farmers in China.

D surplus labor in the countryside.

---

2 A major factor in the settlement of Texas by Anglo-Americans in the late 1800s was

F petroleum.

G the construction of railroads.

H the discovery of gold.

J migration to the Sun Belt.

Geography

Name ______________________ Date ______________ Class __________

TEKS 6B

3 Cecil Rhodes was an important leader in British rule and settlement in southern Africa.

THE RHODES COLOSSUS

STRIDING FROM CAPE TOWN TO CAIRO.

Rhodes developed what resource that attracted settlers to South Africa?

A diamonds

B farmland

C factories

D timber

Check your answers.
If you missed 0, great job!
If you missed 1, not bad.
If you missed 2-3, review the processes that have caused changes in settlement patterns.

Name ______________________ Date ______________ Class __________

TEKS 7A

Choose the best answer for each question. Circle the letter for the correct answer, or record your answer and fill in the bubbles on the provided griddable.

1 This population pyramid represents the United States.

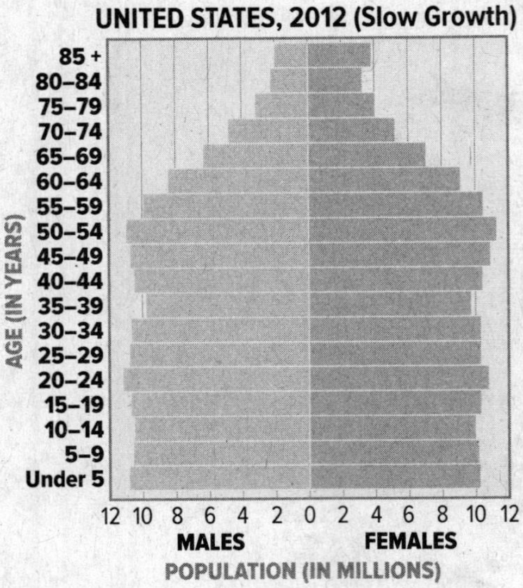

Source: U.S. Census Bureau, Statistical Abstract of the United States: 2012

Which statement best describes the population of the United States?

A Many babies are being born, but few are surviving to adulthood.

B The population is stable, with many people living to old age.

C There is a lot of immigration of young adults.

D Men outlive women.

Geography

Name ______________________ Date ______________ Class ________

TEKS 7A

2 This population pyramid represents Chad.

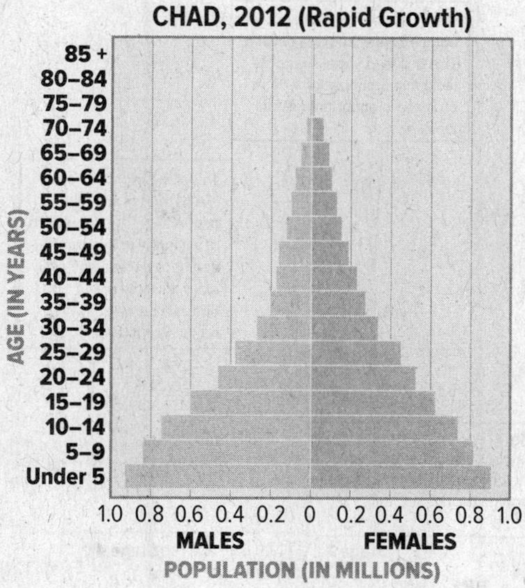

Source: U.S. Census Bureau, Statistical Abstract of the United States: 2012

Chad would be classified as a

F developed country.

G newly industrializing country.

H less developed country.

J wealthy country.

Name ______________________ Date ______________ Class __________

TEKS 7A

3 This graph shows the general pattern of the demographic transition.

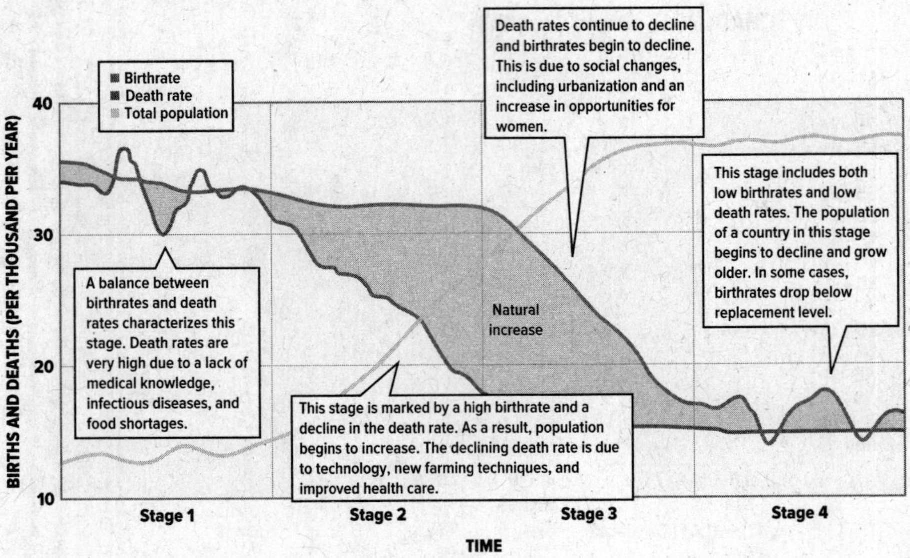

In terms of the demographic transition, the United States is in

A Stage 1.

B Stage 2.

C Stage 3.

D Stage 4.

Check your answers.
If you missed 0, great job!
If you missed 1, not bad.
If you missed 2-3, review population pyramids and other graphics to describe the characteristics of populations and predict future trends.

Name ______________________ Date ____________ Class ________

TEKS 7B

Choose the best answer for each question. Circle the letter for the correct answer, or record your answer and fill in the bubbles on the provided griddable.

1 The primary pull factor in migration to the United States from Latin America is

A religious freedom.

B economic opportunity.

C lax immigration laws.

D mild weather.

---

2 For refugees, the most important cause of migration is

F economic opportunity in a new home.

G the presence of people of the same nationality in a new home.

H intolerable conditions in the present home.

J a government order to move.

Geography

Name ______________________ Date ______________ Class __________

TEKS 7B

Geography

3 The main factor in Arabs becoming refugees in the Eastern Mediterranean is

A the pull factor of economic opportunity.

B the pull factor of religious freedom.

C the push factor of war.

D the push factor of hurricanes.

Check your answers.
If you missed 0, great job!
If you missed 1, not bad.
If you missed 2-3, review how political, economic, social, and environmental push and pull factors affect human migration.

Name ______________________ Date ______________ Class __________

TEKS 7C

Choose the best answer for each question. Circle the letter for the correct answer, or record your answer and fill in the bubbles on the provided griddable.

1 This graph shows the general pattern of the demographic transition.

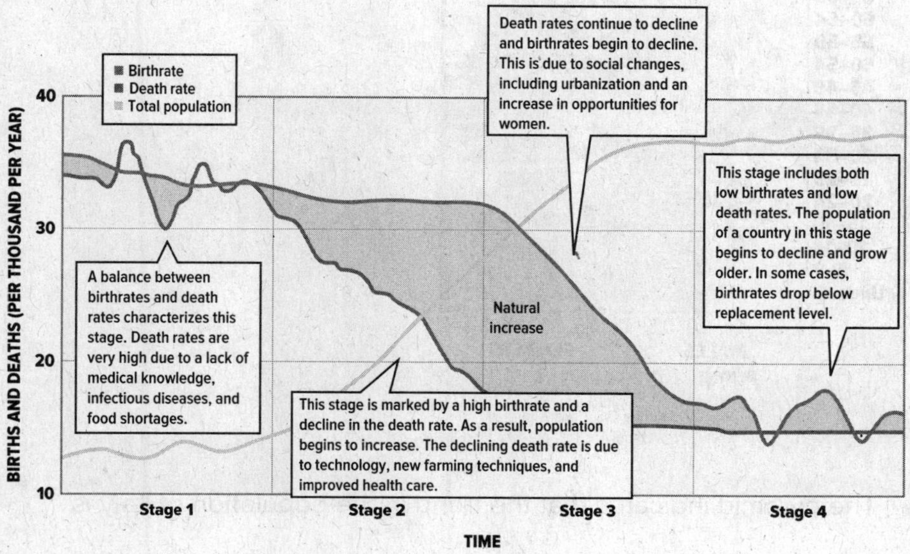

The trend that the model projects indicates that future world population will

A continue to grow rapidly.

B decline.

C continue to grow, but more slowly than it has been recently.

D remain exactly as it is.

Geography

Name ______________________ Date ______________ Class __________

TEKS 7C

2 This pyramid shows the population of Italy.

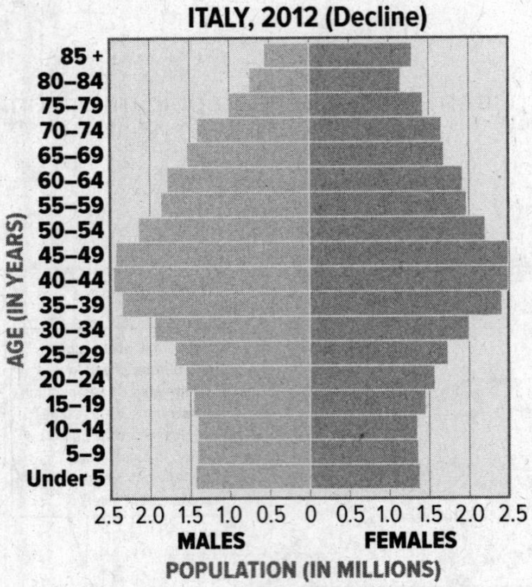

Source: U.S. Census Bureau, Statistical Abstract of the United States: 2012

The pyramid indicates that the trend in the population of Italy is

F the population will decline.

G the population will increase rapidly.

H the population will increase slowly.

J It is impossible to tell from the pyramid.

Name ______________________ Date ______________ Class __________

TEKS 7C

3 This graph shows current population and expected population in 2050 for selected countries.

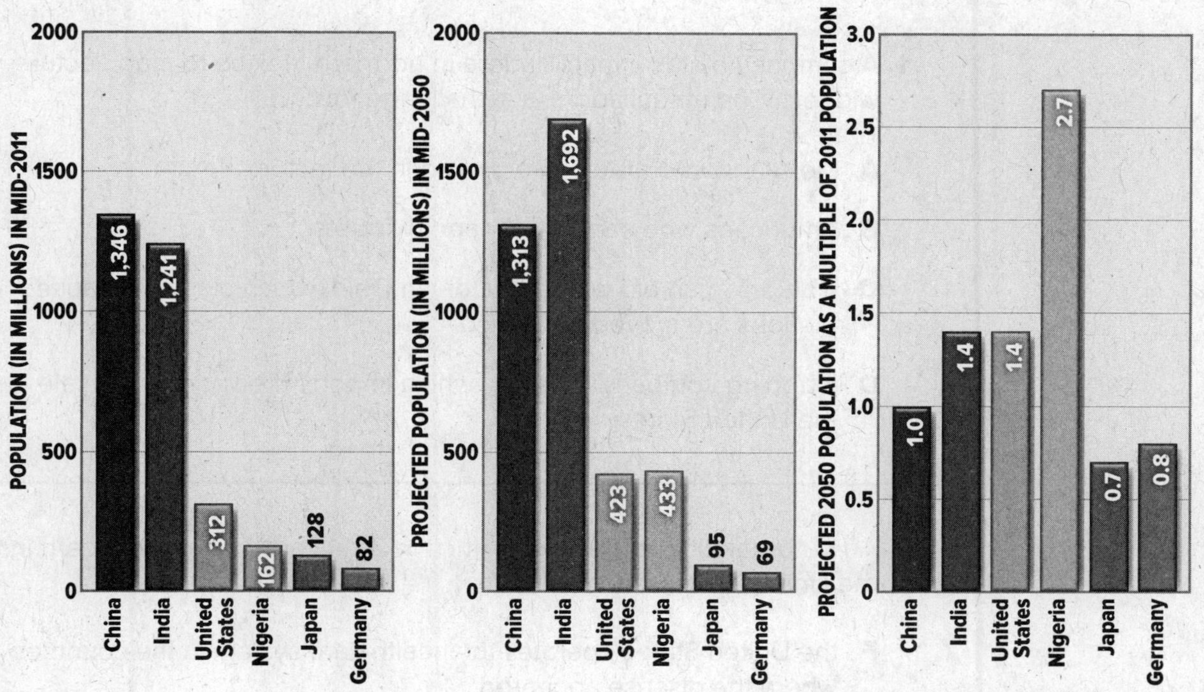

Source: Population Reference Bureau, *2011 World Population Data Sheet*

According to this graph, the fastest rate of growth in population is expected to be in

A the United States.

B Japan.

C India.

D Nigeria.

Check your answers.
If you missed 0, great job!
If you missed 1, not bad.
If you missed 2-3, review how political, economic, social, and environmental push and pull factors affect human migration.

Name ______________________ Date ______________ Class __________

TEKS 7D

Choose the best answer for each question. Circle the letter for the correct answer, or record your answer and fill in the bubbles on the provided griddable.

1 A company builds a maquiladora in northern Mexico to manufacture widgets. The maquiladora is a challenge for

A Mexicans who may be employed in the factory.

B Americans who can buy cheaper widgets.

C workers in an old widget factory in Ohio, which closes because the jobs are moved to Mexico.

D a trading company in Texas, which imports the widgets for sale in the United States.

---

2 An outbreak of Ebola in West Africa in 2014 caused great concern in the United States because

F the United States operates the health-care system in the countries where the disease appeared.

G Americans working in those countries might bring the virus back to the United States.

H the virus is transmitted via ocean currents.

J the illness might cause a civil war in the countries where it appeared.

Geography

Name ______________________ Date ______________ Class __________

TEKS 7D

3 The most important connectivity technology in the Arab Spring was

A the telephone.

B newspapers.

C word of mouth.

D the Internet.

Geography

Check your answers.
If you missed 0, great job!
If you missed 1, not bad.
If you missed 2-3, review the benefits and challenges of globalization

Name ______________________ Date ______________ Class __________

TEKS 8A

Choose the best answer for each question. Circle the letter for the correct answer, or record your answer and fill in the bubbles on the provided griddable.

1 This map shows the location of early culture hearths.

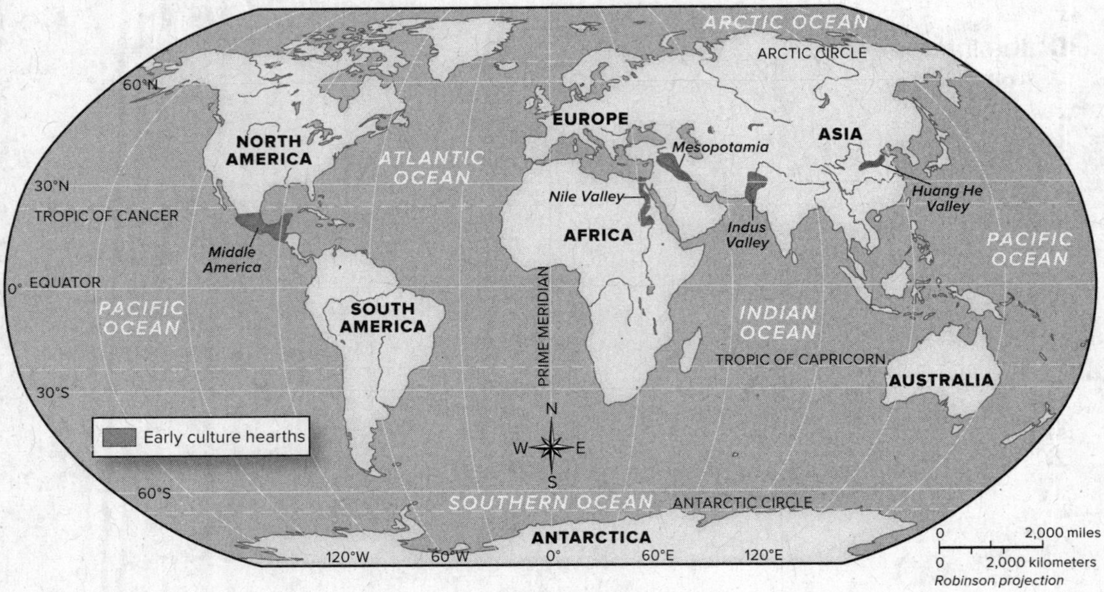

In Asia and Africa, early cultures relied on

A river water for irrigation.

B mountains for mineral wealth.

C grasslands for animal pastures.

D the ocean for world trade.

---

2 Use of resources in the Amazon Basin is changing.

The activity that is responsible for the most deforestation in the Amazon is

F lumbering.

G subsistence farming.

H ranching.

J urbanization.

Name ________________ Date ________________ Class ________

TEKS 8A

3 This map shows predominant economic activities in Texas.

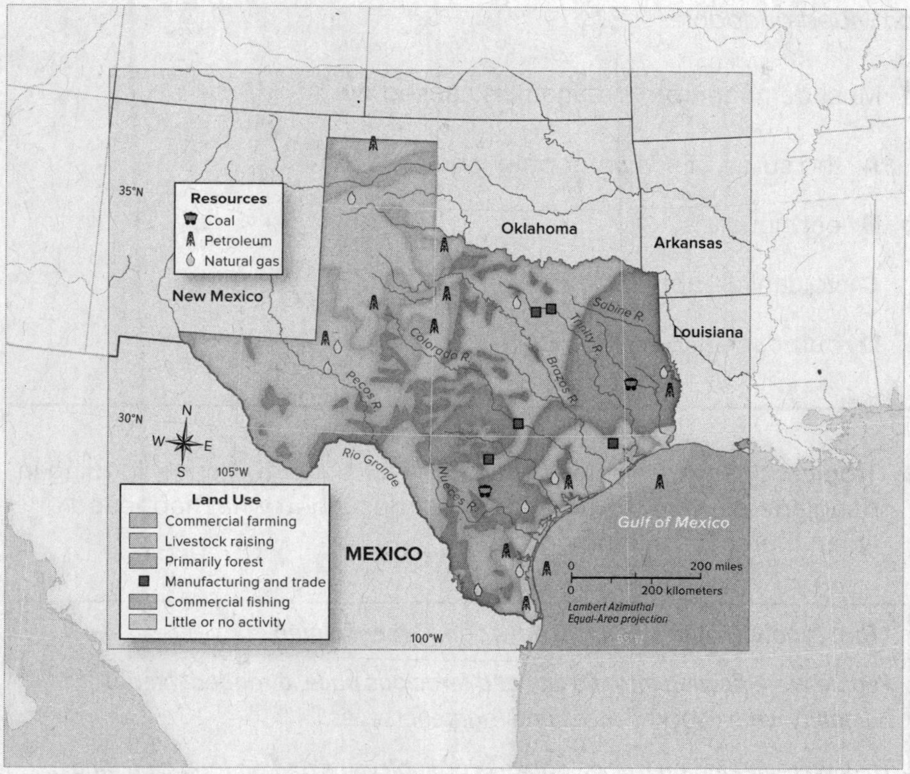

Livestock ranching as well as raising corn and grain sorghum in the High Plains of western Texas depend on the resource of

A irrigation water from the Rio Grande.

B the largest cities in Texas.

C oil wells.

D underground aquifers.

Check your answers.
If you missed 0, great job!
If you missed 1, not bad.
If you missed 2-3, review ways humans depend on, adapt to, and modify the physical environment

Name ______________________ Date ______________ Class __________

TEKS 8B

Choose the best answer for each question. Circle the letter for the correct answer, or record your answer and fill in the bubbles on the provided griddable.

1 Most damage from a tsunami is caused by

A the surge of seawater onto land.

B earthquakes.

C volcanic eruptions.

D hurricane-like storms.

---

2 Tropical cyclones, similar to hurricanes, frequently cause flooding in Bangladesh. Here is how a journalist described what happened when there was a flood.

> ***"That is how I felt in Sukkur 10 days ago. Overwhelmed.***
>
> ***People were flowing into the city at a ferocious pace, a ragged river of humanity, with shocked faces and frightened eyes.***
>
> ***They were fleeing on trucks, donkey carts, bicycles and on foot, clutching whatever was precious—electric fans, bedding, pots and pans, chickens and goats. Behind them, a great***
>
> ***sinister mass of floodwater was pouring in."***
>
> **—Jill McGivering, "'Elation' and 'Unease' at Helping Pakistan Flood Child," *BBC News*, September 4, 2010**

Despite the frequent floods, people in Bangladesh continue to live in lowlands along rivers because

F the country is crowded, and there are no other spaces for living.

G they need the river water to irrigate their crops of rice.

H the government has ordered them to live there.

J they have built a string of large seaports along the rivers.

Name ________________ Date ________ Class ________

TEKS 8B

3 In an El Niño year, atmospheric pressure rises in the Western Pacific and falls in the Eastern Pacific, reversing the normal wind patterns and changing weather over a wide area.

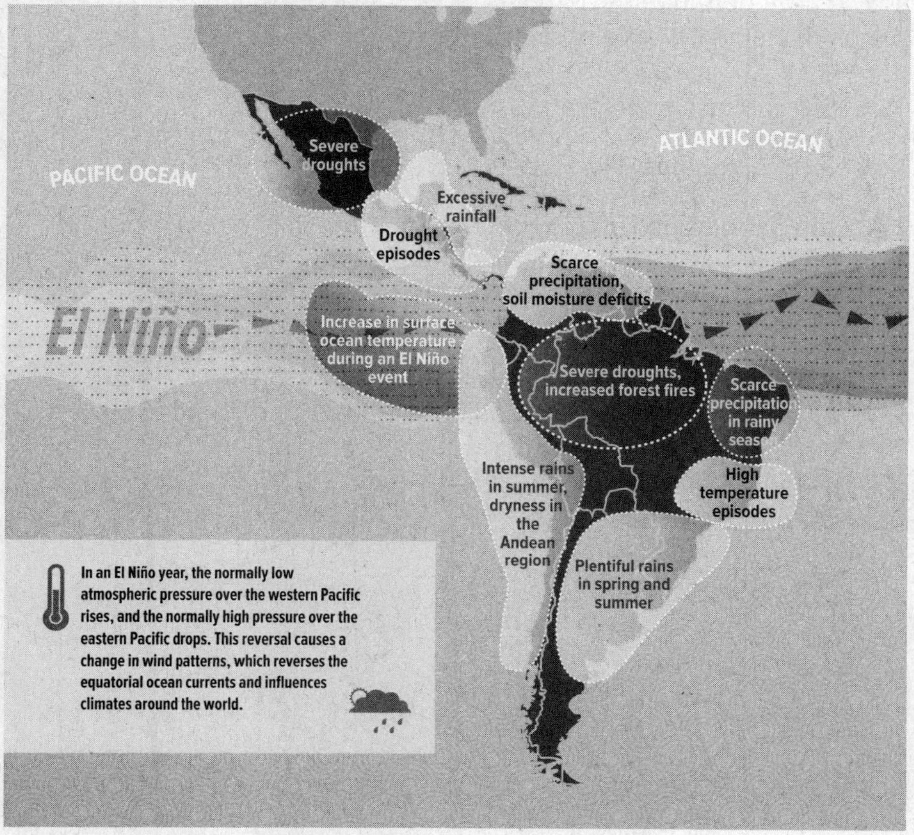

The impact of El Niño in the central South America is

A heavy rain and flooding.

B warmer-than-usual temperatures.

C severe drought.

D colder-than-normal temperatures.

Check your answers.
If you missed 0, great job!
If you missed 1, not bad.
If you missed 2-3, review the consequences of extreme weather and other natural disasters

Name ______________________ Date ______________ Class ________

TEKS 8C

Choose the best answer for each question. Circle the letter for the correct answer, or record your answer and fill in the bubbles on the provided griddable.

1 The area of Bangladesh that is most at risk because of non-sustainable development is

A the capital city of Dhaka.

B the Chittagong Hills.

C the Sundarbans and their mangrove forests.

D farmland.

---

2 The Aral Sea has lost almost all of its water since about 1959.

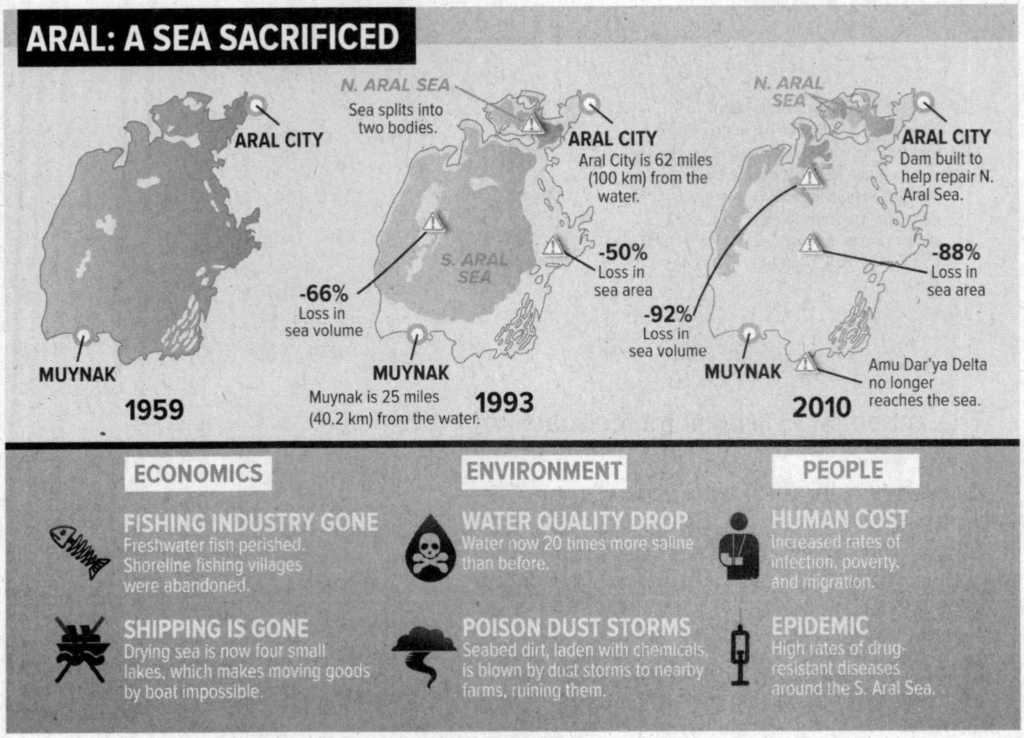

The disappearance of the Aral Sea was primarily the result of

F Soviet government development schemes.

G droughts.

H high temperatures.

J the opening of a new channel that drained the water away.

Name ______________________ Date ______________ Class __________

TEKS 8C

3 In West Africa, tropical hardwoods are an important export, earning income for the countries. If not carried out in a sustainable fashion, the harvesting of these resources can lead to

A massive regrowth of forests, taking away farmland.

B erosion.

C excessive rainfall.

D rural-to-urban migration.

Geography

Check your answers.
If you missed 0, great job!
If you missed 1, not bad.
If you missed 2-3, review sustainable development and renewable/non-renewable resources.

Name ______________________ Date ______________ Class __________

TEKS 9A

Choose the best answer for each question. Circle the letter for the correct answer, or record your answer and fill in the bubbles on the provided griddable.

Geography

1 Although they are separate countries, Myanmar (Burma), Thailand, Laos, Cambodia, and Vietnam share a region based on

A a mountain range.

B rule by the same colonial power.

C the Mekong River.

D their role in the Vietnam War.

---

2 British India included the present-day countries of India, Pakistan, and Bangladesh.

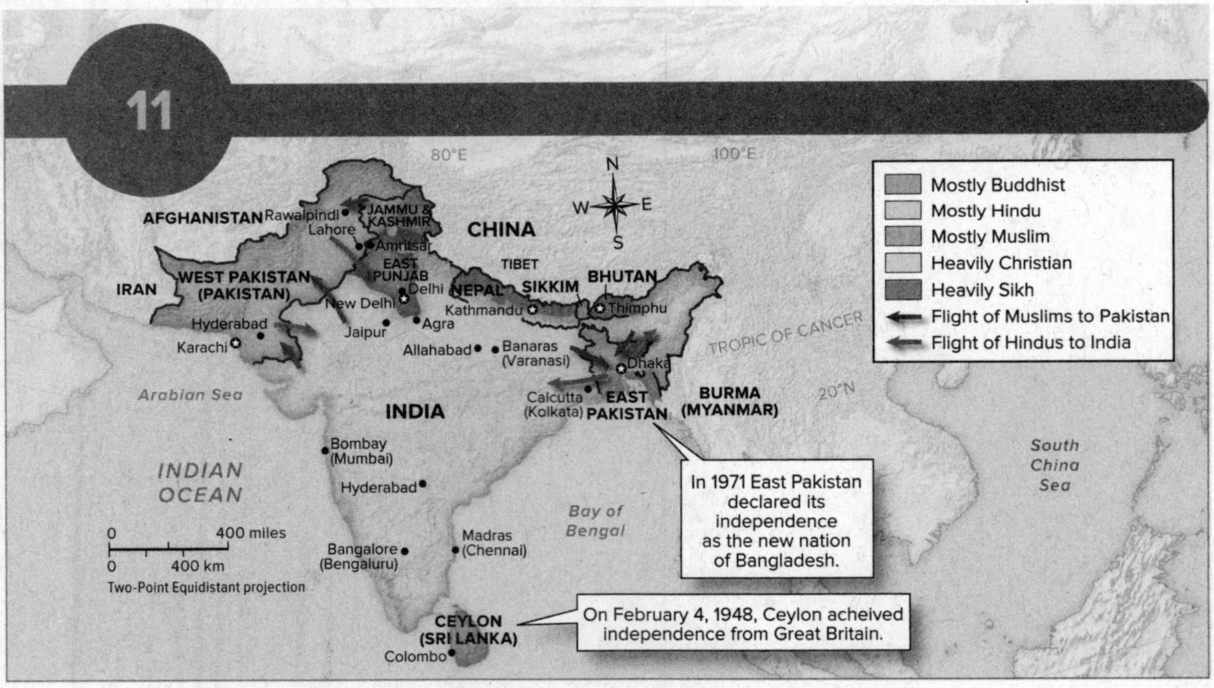

The division of British India into different countries in general followed regions based on

F landforms.

G climate.

H British administrative units.

J religion.

Name ______________________ Date ______________ Class __________

TEKS 9A

3 The Sahel in the African Transition Zone is a region based on

A colonial rule.

B dates of independence.

C a seacoast.

D vegetation.

Geography

Check your answers.
If you missed 0, great job!
If you missed 1, not bad.
If you missed 2-3, review physical and/or human factors that constitute regions.

Name ____________ Date ____________ Class ____________

TEKS 9B

Choose the best answer for each question. Circle the letter for the correct answer, or record your answer and fill in the bubbles on the provided griddable.

1 This map shows the predominant language family in different parts of the world.

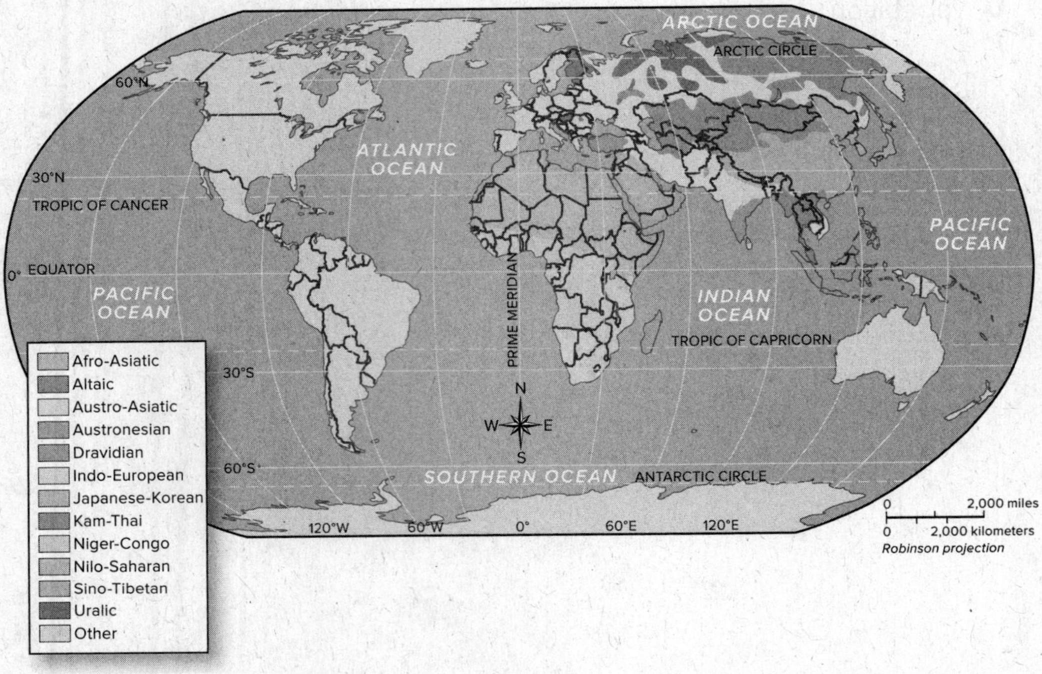

Language regions are an example of

A functional regions.

B formal regions.

C nodal regions.

D perceptual regions.

---

2 The region from which people commute to jobs in Houston is an example of a

F functional region.

G formal region.

H perceptual region.

J cultural region.

Name ______________________ Date ______________ Class ________

TEKS 9B

3 Although the Piney Woods of Texas is based on the presence of a type of vegetation, it is also a

A climate region.

B perceptual region.

C functional region.

D formal region.

Geography

Check your answers.
If you missed 0, great job!
If you missed 1, not bad.
If you missed 2-3, review types of regions.

Name ______________________ Date ______________ Class __________

TEKS 10A

Choose the best answer for each question. Circle the letter for the correct answer, or record your answer and fill in the bubbles on the provided griddable.

1 In a free enterprise economic system, major decisions about what to produce and how, and to whom the products go are made by

A the government.

B private individuals.

C farmers.

D computers.

---

2 An economic system in which the state owns all means of production and determines what will be produced and who will receive the results is

F socialism.

G communism.

H free enterprise.

J a mixed economy.

Name ______________________ Date ______________ Class __________

TEKS 10A

3 An economic system in which the government owns basic economic activities and provides basic services to the population, while other activity is privately owned, is

A communism.

B free market.

C socialism.

D a command economy.

Economics

Check your answers.
If you missed 0, great job!
If you missed 1, not bad.
If you missed 2-3, review forces that determine the distribution of goods and services in various types of economic systems.

Name ______________________ Date ______________ Class __________

TEKS 10B

Choose the best answer for each question. Circle the letter for the correct answer, or record your answer and fill in the bubbles on the provided griddable.

1 In the 1980s, China adopted major reforms of its economic system. It moved

A from communism to capitalism.

B from capitalism to communism.

C from communism to a mixed economy with more free-market characteristics.

D from a free market to socialism.

---

2 Countries in Northwestern Europe operate schools, universities, and health-care institutions for their people, while allowing them to own businesses and choose their jobs. They illustrate an economic system that is

F mixed socialism and free market.

G mixed socialism and communism.

H purely socialist.

J purely free market.

Name ______________ Date ______________ Class ______________

TEKS 10B

3 Probably the most rigidly communist country in the world today is

A Vietnam.

B China.

C Cuba.

D North Korea.

Economics

Check your answers.
If you missed 0, great job!
If you missed 1, not bad.
If you missed 2-3, review where specific countries lie on the continuum free enterprise and communism.

Name ______________________ Date ______________ Class __________

TEKS 10C

Choose the best answer for each question. Circle the letter for the correct answer, or record your answer and fill in the bubbles on the provided griddable.

1 A farm family in Kenya raises grain, vegetables, and a few chickens. They store the harvest to provide their food supply for the year, until the next harvest. They are engaging in

A commercial farming.

B plantation agriculture.

C subsistence farming.

D globalization.

---

2 A family in Mexico makes traditional crafts at home to sell on a nearby street. They are engaging in

F subsistence farming.

G commercial industry.

H cottage industry.

J tourism.

Economics

Name ________________________ Date ______________ Class ________

TEKS 10C

3 A mark of a newly industrializing country is the shift of more workers

A from farming to commercial industry.

B from commercial industry to knowledge industries.

C into tourism.

D from commercial industry to farming.

Economics

Check your answers.
If you missed 0, great job!
If you missed 1, not bad.
If you missed 2-3, review ways people satisfy basic needs

Name ______________________ Date ______________ Class ________

TEKS 10D

Choose the best answer for each question. Circle the letter for the correct answer, or record your answer and fill in the bubbles on the provided griddable.

1 India has many highly educated, English-speaking computer scientists. American technology companies have established offices where these scientists develop computer software for export to the United States. This is an example of

A outsourcing.

B cottage industry.

C trade barriers.

D localization.

---

2 Among China's reforms in the 1980s that spurred its international trade was

F communes.

G the Red Guards.

H state-owned industry.

J free-trade zones.

Name ______________________ Date ______________ Class __________

TEKS 10D

3 The Crusades were an early instance of globalization because they

A resulted in the conquest of Muslim states in the Eastern Mediterranean by European Christian forces.

B made English a world language.

C opened trade routes between Europe and Asia.

D led to outsourcing to European manufacturing.

Check your answers.
If you missed 0, great job!
If you missed 1, not bad.
If you missed 2-3, review global trade patterns over time

Economics

TEKS 11A

Choose the best answer for each question. Circle the letter for the correct answer, or record your answer and fill in the bubbles on the provided griddable.

1 This table shows the proportion of the gross domestic product (GDP) of several countries that comes from different kinds of economic activity.

Country	Primary	Secondary	Tertiary
A	2	31	67
B	4	37	59
C	31	43	26
D	35	24	41

Data source: CIA World Factbook, http://www.cia.gov/library/publications/the-world-factbook

Which country has the lowest level of economic development?

A Country A

B Country B

C Country C

D Country D

2 Using the same table, which country has the highest level of development?

F Country A

G Country B

H Country C

J Country D

Economics

Name ______________________ Date ______________ Class __________

TEKS 11A

3 Using the same table, which country would you expect to have the highest level of quaternary activity?

A Country A

B Country B

C Country C

D Country D

Economics

Check your answers.
If you missed 0, great job!
If you missed 1, not bad.
If you missed 2-3, review connections between levels of development and economic activities

Name ______________________ Date ______________ Class __________

TEKS 11B

Choose the best answer for each question. Circle the letter for the correct answer, or record your answer and fill in the bubbles on the provided griddable.

1 This map shows economic activities in Texas.

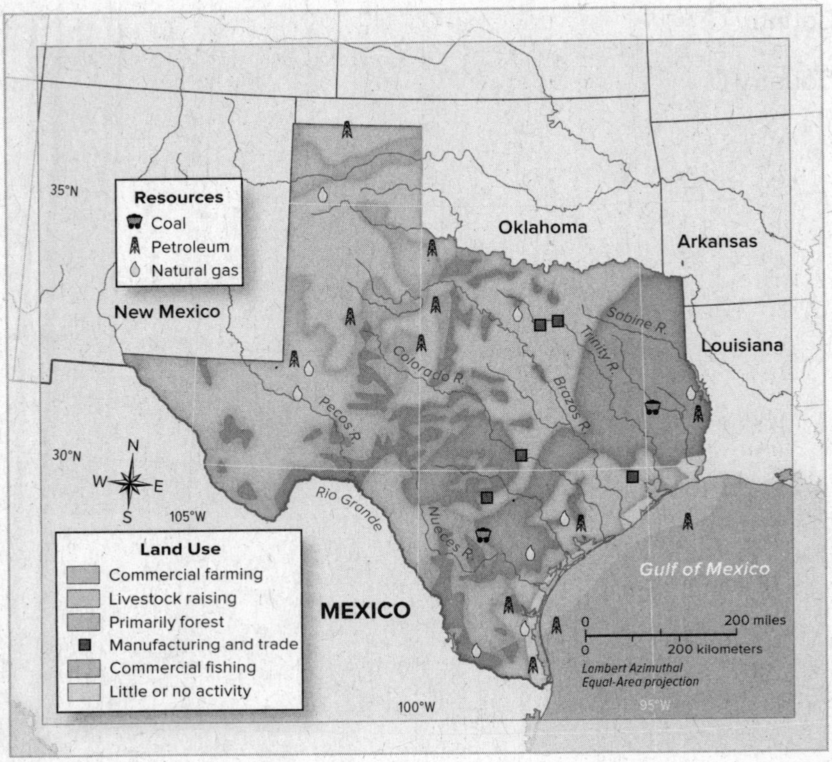

Livestock ranching is primarily located in the part of Texas that

A has large cities.

B is forested.

C has higher rainfall.

D has lower rainfall.

Name ____________ Date ____________ Class ____________

TEKS 11B

2 When China opened to foreign investment in factories in the 1980s, it designated areas along the southeastern coast for this activity. These locations had the advantage that they

F were close to the capital of the country.

G were close to coal mines.

H were convenient for shipping products to foreign markets.

J would take up little farmland for factory construction.

3 When manufacturing activity in the United States spread from its early start in the Northeast, it was attracted by

A large populations for a labor supply in the Midwest.

B large numbers of slaves in the South.

C deposits of coal and iron ore in the Midwest.

D access to markets in Canada.

Economics

Check your answers.
If you missed 0, great job!
If you missed 1, not bad.
If you missed 2-3, review factors affecting the location of different types of economic activities

Name ______________________ Date ______________ Class ________

TEKS 11C

Choose the best answer for each question. Circle the letter for the correct answer, or record your answer and fill in the bubbles on the provided griddable.

1 Farming in the Great Plains of the United States became more feasible in the late 1800s with the invention of

A windmills and barbed wire.

B irrigation canals.

C interstate highways.

D new methods of surveying land.

---

2 Construction of the Trans-Siberian Railway across Russia in the late 1800s opened the Pacific coast of that country to settlement. It also spurred

F tourism in Siberia.

G export of mineral resources from Siberia.

H global warming.

J highway construction.

Name ______________________ Date ____________ Class ________

TEKS 11C

3 This photograph was taken from outer space and shows the Nile River and its delta.

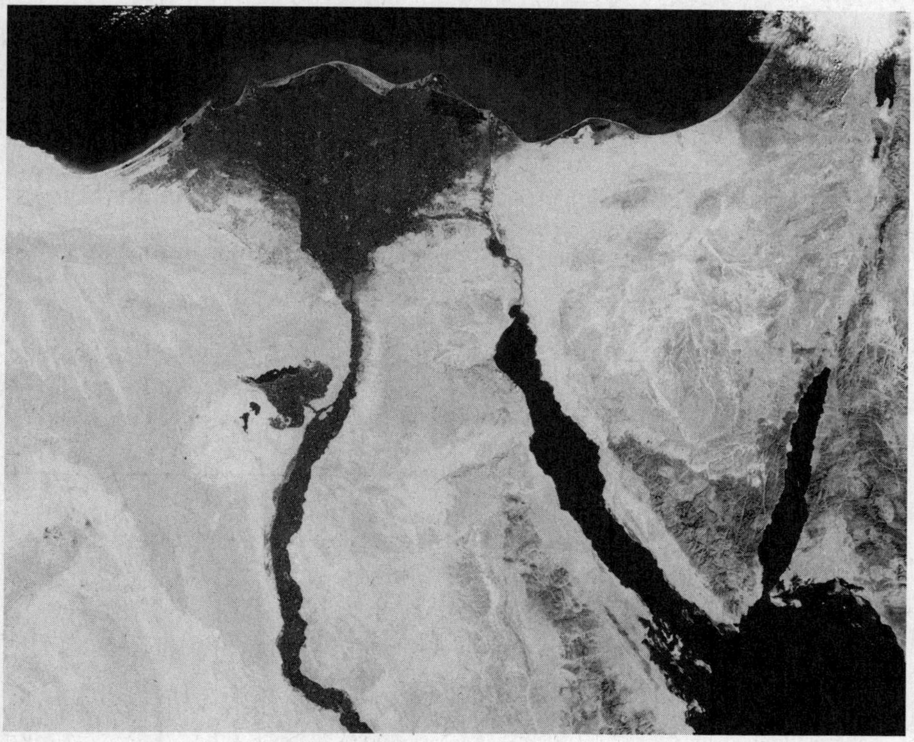

The Nile River became the location of an early civilization in ancient times because

A it contained resources of gold and silver.

B the surrounding desert became drier, and people were seeking water.

C sea level rose, and people needed dry land.

D it was located next to another center of dense population, and people needed more land.

Economics

Check your answers.
If you missed 0, great job!
If you missed 1, not bad.
If you missed 2-3, review how changes in climate, resources and infrastructure affect location and patterns of economic activities.

Name ______________________ Date ______________ Class __________

TEKS 12A

Choose the best answer for each question. Circle the letter for the correct answer, or record your answer and fill in the bubbles on the provided griddable.

1 Burning coal produces air pollution. Consequently, many power plants in the United States have switched to natural gas, which burns cleaner. The result for the coal-mining industry has been

A a decline jobs, leading to out-migration from coal-mining regions.

B an increase in demand, as overseas markets have replaced domestic markets.

C exhaustion of coal resources.

D loosening of regulations regarding pollution.

---

2 Beginning in the 1960s, oil and gas reserves were discovered in Canada's Prairie Provinces. A result has been

F out-migration from the pollution of oil drilling.

G in-migration of people seeking jobs.

H reforestation projects.

J a decline in gasoline prices in Canada.

Name ______________________ Date ______________ Class __________

TEKS 12A

3 To generate more electricity and control flooding, China built the huge Three Gorges Dam on the Chang Jiang (Yangtze River).

A consequence of this project is

A a new city at the base of the dam.

B the relocation of at least 1 million people who formerly lived where the reservoir is now.

C increased flooding downstream of the dam.

D climate change.

Check your answers.
If you missed 0, great job!
If you missed 1, not bad.
If you missed 2-3, review how changes in key natural resources affect movement of products, money, and people.

Economics

Name ______________________ Date ______________ Class __________

TEKS 12B

Choose the best answer for each question. Circle the letter for the correct answer, or record your answer and fill in the bubbles on the provided griddable.

1 The California State Water Project was built to

A increase rainfall.

B provide water for California's residences and farms.

C build water parks.

D encourage water conservation.

---

2 The Suez Canal was built in the 1800s to provide a more direct shipping route from Europe to Asia. Its effect on the Mediterranean Sea has been

F an increase in invasive species.

G rising numbers of tourists.

H increased fishing.

J boundary disputes.

Name ______________________ Date ______________ Class __________

TEKS 12B

3 In a policy aimed at sustainable development, the Philippines and Malaysia have

A encouraged the establishment of palm oil plantations.

B limited certain timber exports.

C required payment of a tax on mine products.

D controlled rural-to-urban migration.

Economics

Check your answers.
If you missed 0, great job!
If you missed 1, not bad.
If you missed 2-3, review the geographic and economic impact of policies related to development.

Name ______________________ Date ______________ Class __________

TEKS 13A

Choose the best answer for each question. Circle the letter for the correct answer, or record your answer and fill in the bubbles on the provided griddable.

1 This map shows physical features and regions of Texas.

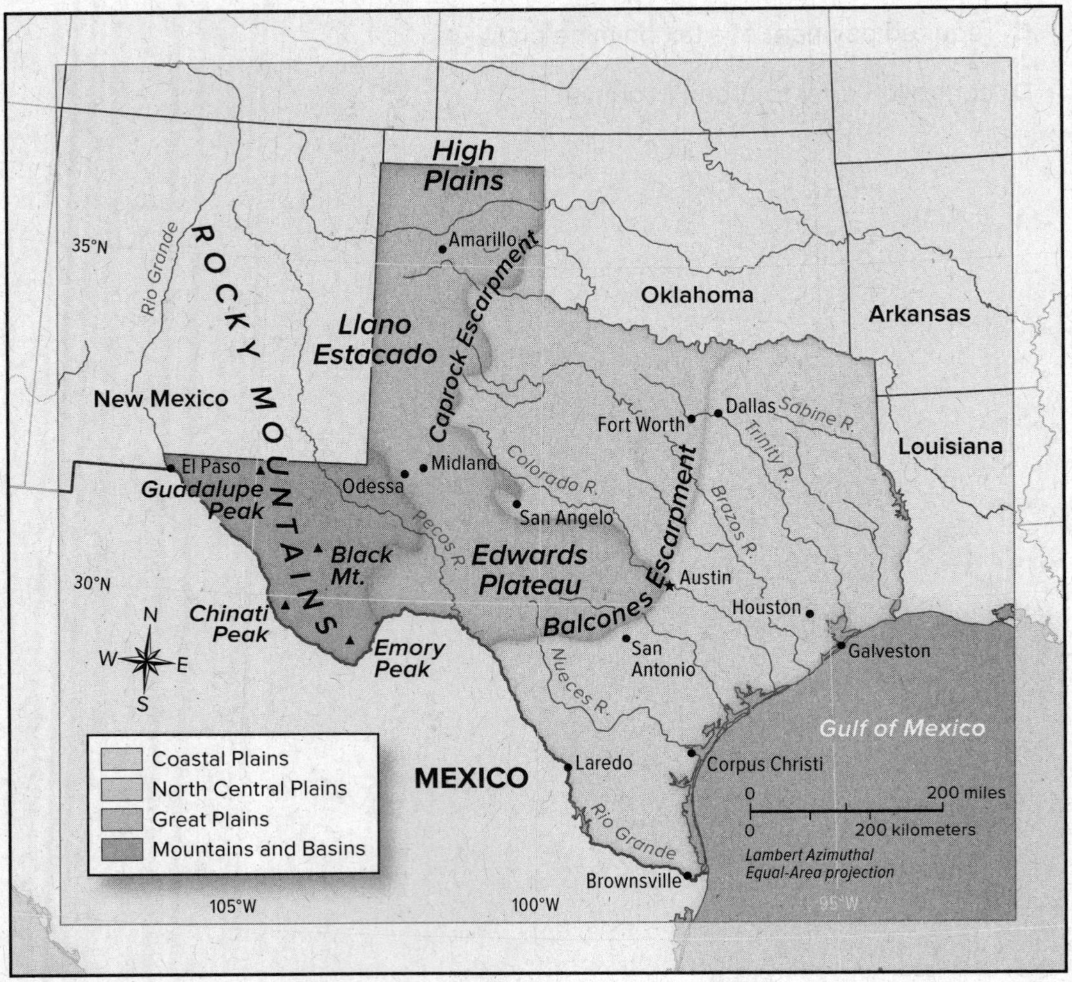

A physical boundary of the state of Texas is

A the Balcones Escarpment.

B the Rio Grande.

C the Rocky Mountains.

D the Edwards Plateau.

Name ______________________ Date ______________ Class ____________

TEKS 13A

2 This map shows the present-day countries of Africa and the dates of their independence.

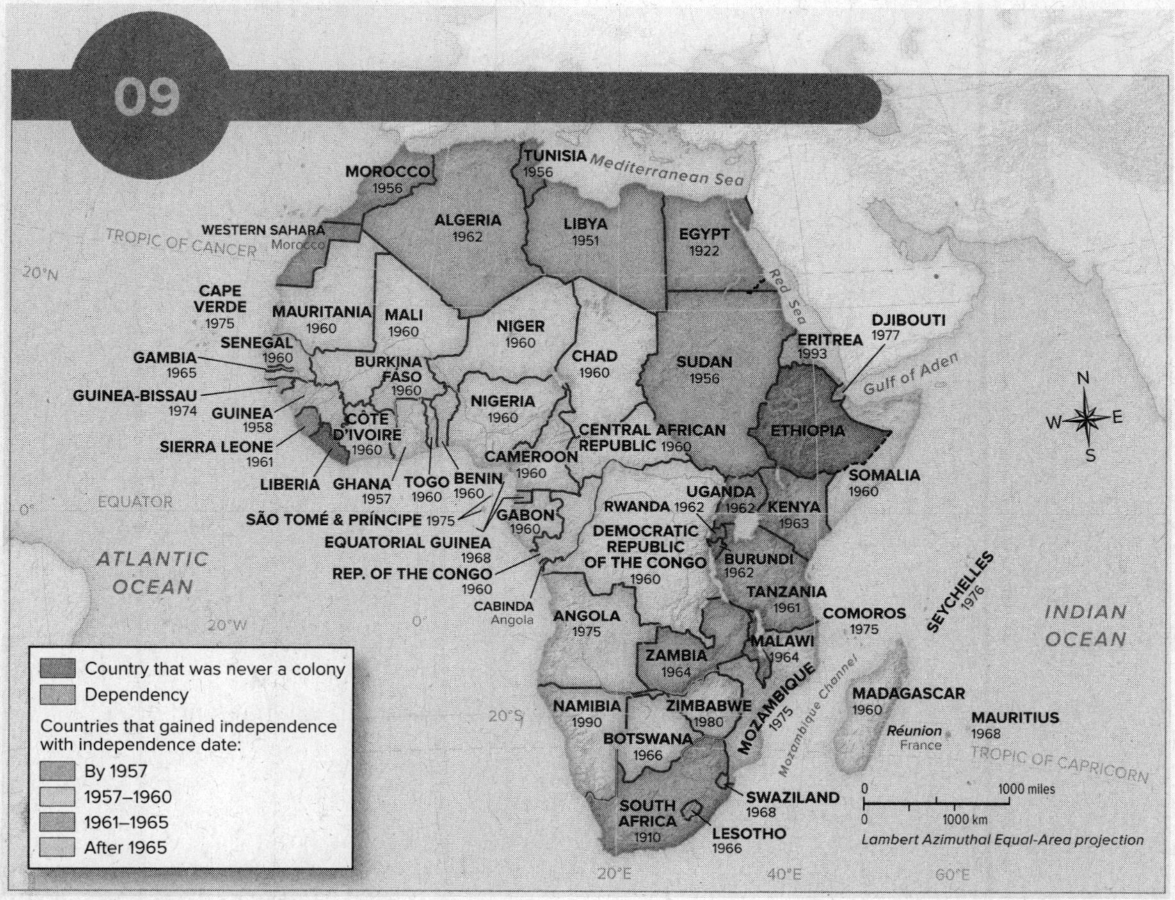

The southern boundary of Egypt is what kind of boundary?

F a cultural boundary

G a physical boundary

H an antecedent boundary

J a geometric boundary

Name ______ Date ______ Class ______

TEKS 13A

3 This map shows physical features and boundaries in Southeast Asia.

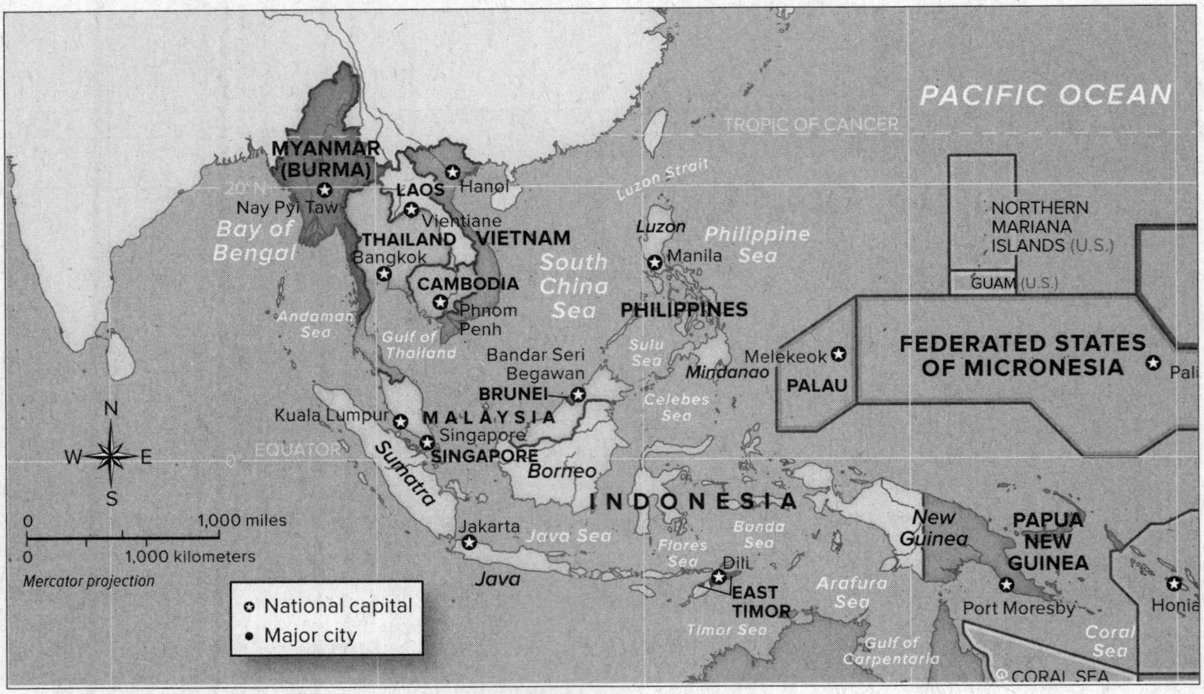

The eastern boundary of Burma (Myanmar) is what kind of boundary?

A physical boundary

B antecedent boundary

C geometric boundary

D relict boundary

Government

Check your answers.
If you missed 0, great job!
If you missed 1, not bad.
If you missed 2-3, review the division of land by man-made and natural boundaries.

Name ______________________ Date ______________ Class ________

TEKS 13B

Choose the best answer for each question. Circle the letter for the correct answer, or record your answer and fill in the bubbles on the provided griddable.

1 The map on the left shows the boundaries of the congressional districts in Ohio in 2010. After the 2010 census was taken, Ohio lost a representative in Congress, so the boundaries had to be redrawn to reduce the number of districts from 17 to 16. The map on the right shows the proposed boundaries.

Ohio Districts, 2010

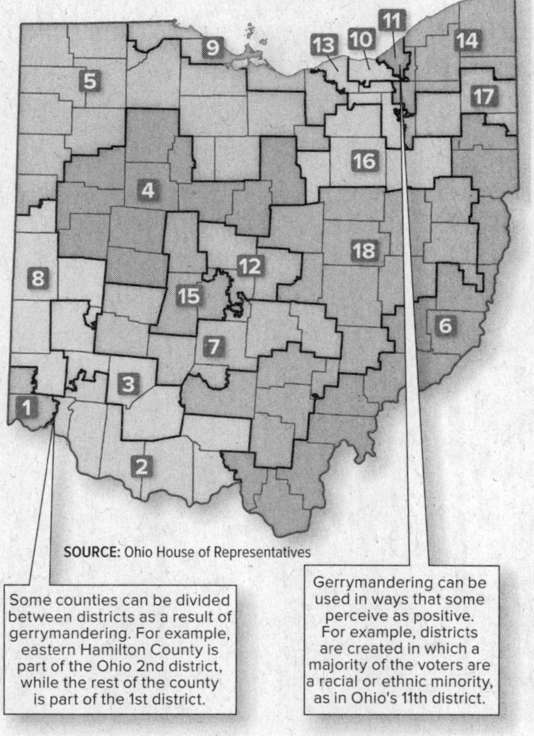

Proposed Districts in Ohio

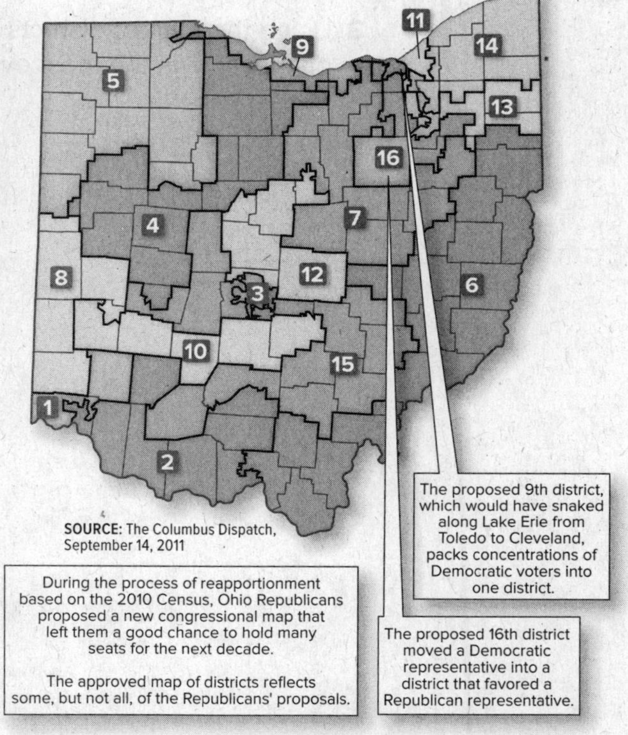

District 5 in northwestern Ohio covers more area than District 1 in southwest Ohio because

A they are gerrymandered.

B District 5 is more sparsely populated than District 1.

C District 1 was settled earlier than District 5.

D District 5 has two representatives.

Government

Name ______________________ Date ______________ Class ________

TEKS 13B

2 Using the map of proposed districts, which district shows the least evidence of gerrymandering?

F District 11

G District 8

H District 3

J District 9

---

3 Using the map of districts in 2010 (before they were redrawn), which district shows the most evidence of gerrymandering?

A District 12

B District 13

C District 11

D District 15

Check your answers.
If you missed 0, great job!
If you missed 1, not bad.
If you missed 2-3, review how maps of political boundaries show evidence of voting power.

Government

Name ______________________ Date ______________ Class __________

TEKS 14A

Choose the best answer for each question. Circle the letter for the correct answer, or record your answer and fill in the bubbles on the provided griddable.

1 Which part of Ukraine has been seized by Russia, on the basis that a large portion of its people are Russian?

A Transdniestria

B Kiev

C Crimea

D Chernobyl

---

2 South Sudan seceded from Sudan and became a new country in 2011, based on

F differences in language and religion.

G a desire for more seats in the United Nations.

H a directive by China.

J greater access to oil resources by two countries than one.

Name ____________________ Date ____________ Class __________

TEKS 14A

3 After 45 years of division, Germany was reunited in 1990.

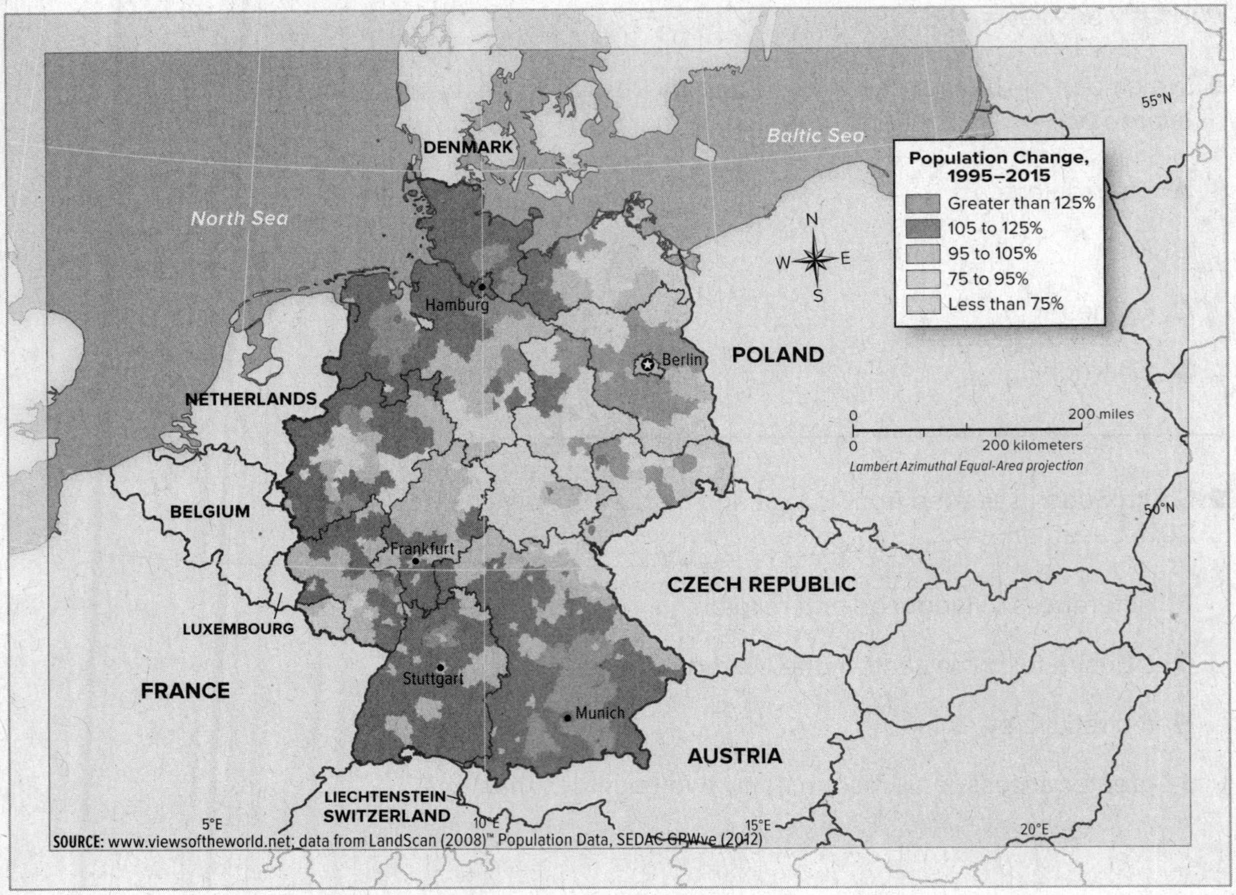

Although Germany was reunited in 1990, this map shows that the part that was under Communist rule is still evident in

A religious divisions.

B votes for the Communist party.

C population growth rates.

D education levels.

Check your answers.
If you missed 0, great job!
If you missed 1, not bad.
If you missed 2-3, review physical and human processes that lead to boundaries and other divisions.

Name ______________________ Date ______________ Class __________

TEKS 14B

Choose the best answer for each question. Circle the letter for the correct answer, or record your answer and fill in the bubbles on the provided griddable.

1 Canada, the United Kingdom, and Australia recognize the monarch of the United Kingdom as head of state. Their kind of government is

A dictatorship.

B constitutional monarchy.

C republic.

D theocracy.

---

2 In 1979 a revolution in Iran established a government that is a

F monarchy.

G republic.

H democracy.

J theocracy.

Name ____________________ Date ____________ Class ________

TEKS 14B

3 North Korea's government is

A a democracy.

B a republic.

C a theocracy.

D totalitarian.

Government

Check your answers.
If you missed 0, great job!
If you missed 1, not bad.
If you missed 2-3, review how different types of government systems operate in different countries.

Name ______________________ Date ______________ Class __________

TEKS 14C

Choose the best answer for each question. Circle the letter for the correct answer, or record your answer and fill in the bubbles on the provided griddable.

1 Despite having fought a war with each other in the 1980s, Iran and Iraq together have considerable influence over flows of money among countries of the world through their membership in

A OPEC.

B the European Union.

C the United Nations.

D Doctors without Borders.

---

2 What became the European Union began with agreements regarding

F a common currency.

G oil and gas.

H coal and iron.

J the European Parliament.

Name ______________________ Date ______________ Class __________

TEKS 14C

3 The United States allowed China to join the World Trade Organization to encourage that country to

A develop its manufacturing sector.

B produce more rice.

C improve its human rights record.

D designate more Special Economic Zones.

Government

Check your answers.
If you missed 0, great job!
If you missed 1, not bad.
If you missed 2-3, review factors that influence the power to control territory and resources.

Name ____________________ Date ____________ Class ________

TEKS 15A

Choose the best answer for each question. Circle the letter for the correct answer, or record your answer and fill in the bubbles on the provided griddable.

1 In New Orleans, levees have been built to keep water from the sea and from the Mississippi River from flooding the city. An argument by environmentalists against building such levees is that

A the levees are ugly.

B the levees make it hard for people to enjoy the waterfront.

C the levees prevent the deposition of silt from the river and thus contribute to the city sinking farther below sea level.

D the levees cost too much.

---

2 The federal government requires that motor vehicles sold in the United States meet standards of efficiency in fuel use. An economic argument against such standards is that they

F encourage people to buy cars built in other countries.

G make cars more expensive, so that people will not buy them and auto workers will lose their jobs.

H make gasoline more expensive.

J raise the cost of building highways.

Name ______________________ Date ______________ Class __________

TEKS 15A

3 China resists other countries' desires that it improve the human rights of its people because it believes that such policies are not the business of foreigners. The United States and other countries have argued that

A all countries have a right to do as they please within their own borders.

B Americans want the Chinese people to become just like them.

C all people everywhere have certain basic human rights, which all governments must respect.

D the Chinese are incapable of governing their country appropriately.

Check your answers.
If you missed 0, great job!
If you missed 1, not bad.
If you missed 2-3, review points of view that influence decision-making.

Name ______________________ Date ______________ Class __________

TEKS 15B

Choose the best answer for each question. Circle the letter for the correct answer, or record your answer and fill in the bubbles on the provided griddable.

1 In many Muslim countries of Southwestern Asia, decisions about political issues are based on

A sharia law.

B the United Nations.

C a constitution.

D ancient Roman law.

---

2 A newspaper article about climate change and global warming stated

> ***"As David McCabe, an atmospheric scientist with the Clean Air Task Force explains, many of the half-dozen recent studies that have tried to compare coal with natural gas are plagued by questionable assumptions and flaws. 'From the best of the collective work,' McCabe notes, 'we believe that burning natural gas for electricity produces about 30–50% less greenhouse gas than burning coal.' But that's not a definitive number, and more research needs to be done here."***
>
> **—Brad Plumer, "Can natural gas help tackle global warming? A primer," *Washington Post,* August 20, 2012**

According to David McCabe, an atmospheric scientist with the Clean Air Task Force,

F more scientific research is needed to determine the effects of different kinds of fuel on climate change.

G people will decide which fuel to use based on their personal values.

H burning coal is unpatriotic.

J using natural gas instead of coal will completely solve the problem of climate change.

Name ______________________ Date ______________ Class __________

TEKS 15B

3 Countries in Africa became independent in the late 1900s.

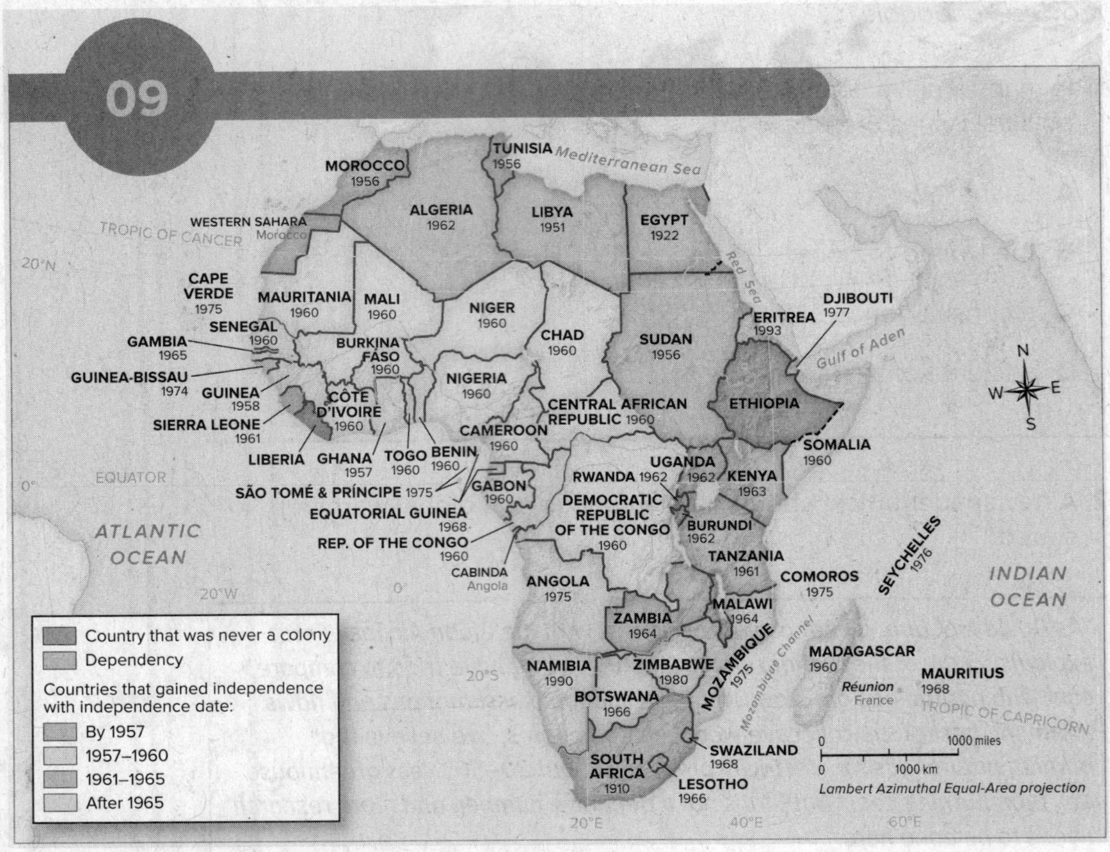

Europeans advanced the decision of Africans to seek independence by

A establishing schools that taught independence.

B being an example of the concept of nationalism into their colonies.

C building factories in African colonies.

D spreading European languages and religions.

Check your answers.
If you missed 0, great job!
If you missed 1, not bad.
If you missed 2-3, review how cultural beliefs influence citizenship practices and decisions.

Citizenship

Name ______________________ Date ______________ Class ________

TEKS 16A

Choose the best answer for each question. Circle the letter for the correct answer, or record your answer and fill in the bubbles on the provided griddable.

1 An important historic landmark in Texas is the Alamo.

Besides its role in Texas's War for Independence, the presence of the Alamo shows

A a history of Spanish settlement in southern Texas.

B the persistence over time of a well-built structure.

C adaptive reuse of buildings.

D a tourist destination.

Name ______________________ Date ______________ Class __________

TEKS 16A

2 This drawing shows the states drawn to a size to match the percentage of their populations who are of Asian ethnic groups.

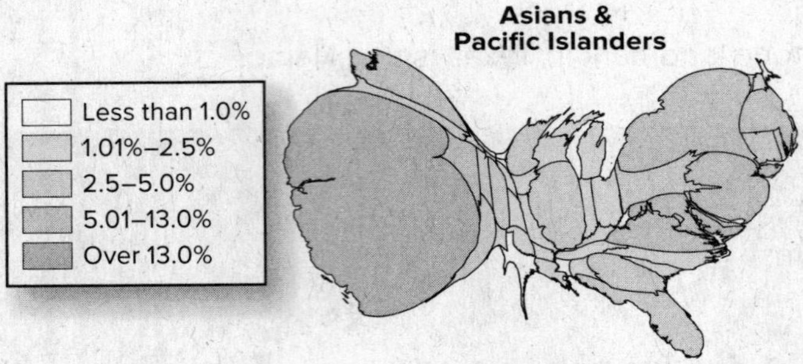

SOURCE: U.S. Census Bureau, 2009

Where would you expect to find a new institution for an Asian religion?

F Tennessee

G Texas

H Ohio

J California

Culture

Name ______________________ Date ______________ Class __________

TEKS 16A

3 The European Union has 24 official languages. The United States, which is about the same size, has one predominant language, although some of its citizens speak other languages. Which statement most accurately describes how innovations spread in the two areas?

A Ideas spread faster in the United States because it has one predominant language.

B Ideas spread faster in the European Union because people are exposed to many languages.

C Ideas spread faster in the European Union because those countries have better public transportation systems.

D Innovations spread at exactly the same speed in both regions.

Culture

Check your answers.
If you missed 0, great job!
If you missed 1, not bad.
If you missed 2-3, review cultural patterns and landscapes and their impact on diffusion.

Name ________________ Date ________________ Class ________

TEKS 16B

Culture

Choose the best answer for each question. Circle the letter for the correct answer, or record your answer and fill in the bubbles on the provided griddable.

1 A variety of a language that may include differences in pronunciation and vocabulary is

A an official language.

B a dialect.

C a language family.

D a dead language.

---

2 The most important social institution in all cultures is

F the government.

G schools.

H the family.

J industry.

Name ______________________ Date ______________ Class __________

TEKS 16B

3 The cultural element that describes how cultures meet daily needs is

A the government.

B the family.

C religion.

D the economy.

Check your answers.
If you missed 0, great job!
If you missed 1, not bad.
If you missed 2-3, review elements of culture.

Name ______________________ Date ______________ Class ____________

TEKS 16C

Culture

Choose the best answer for each question. Circle the letter for the correct answer, or record your answer and fill in the bubbles on the provided griddable.

1 By 1880, Native Americans in Texas were living on reservations. Which of these statements most accurately reflects the government's perception of Native Americans that led to the establishment of reservations?

A Native American culture required protection of the reservation in order to survive.

B Native Americans could make a better living on a reservation, away from other peoples.

C Native Americans posed a danger to other settlers and needed to be confined where they could be controlled.

D Native American reservations would be popular tourist attractions.

---

2 Europeans established trade routes with China beginning in the 1600s as they explored other parts of the world. The Chinese response to these contacts with other cultures was

F to welcome the opportunity to increase trade.

G to resist European traders until forced to open to Westerners in the 1800s.

H to ally with the Japanese to resist the Westerners.

J to ally with the United States to protect their culture.

Name ______________________ Date ______________ Class __________

TEKS 16C

3 In the late 1800s European colonial powers divided Africa into colonies.

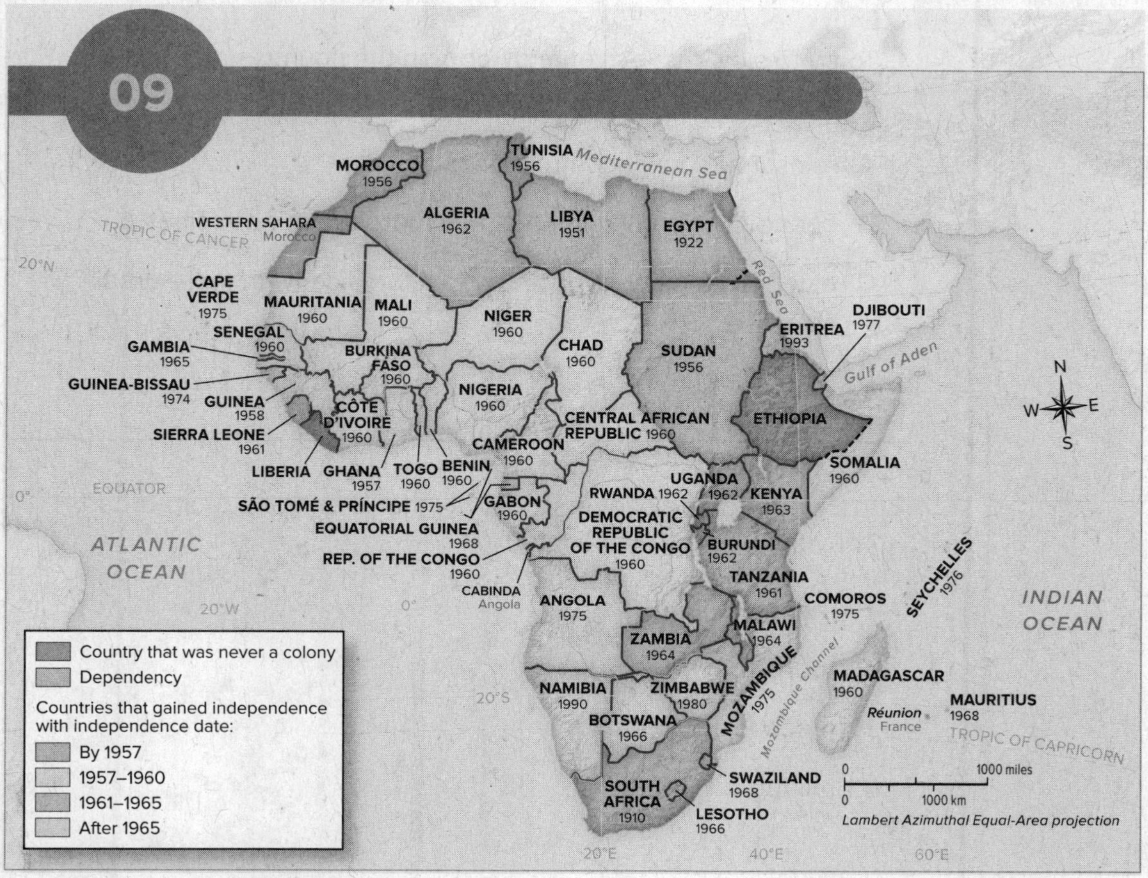

Which of these statements best describes the role of Africans in the division?

A African delegates worked with Europeans at the Berlin conference that created the maps.

B Africans had no say in how the land was divided.

C People who had explored Africa conveyed the views of Africans to the participants at the Berlin conference.

D After the maps were proposed, Africans voted on the division of land.

Check your answers.
If you missed 0, great job!
If you missed 1, not bad.
If you missed 2-3, review how people perceive their own and other cultures differently.

Name ______________________________ Date ____________________ Class __________

TEKS 16D

Choose the best answer for each question. Circle the letter for the correct answer, or record your answer and fill in the bubbles on the provided griddable.

1 To try to slow the loss of farm labor in the countryside from migration to cities, the Chinese government has

A reinstituted strict controls on migration.

B banned the construction of any more factories in cities.

C established new towns in the countryside, with more urban services.

D raised the pay of farm workers.

---

2 In East Africa, an economic activity that is bringing more urban conveniences to the countryside is

F manufacturing.

G tourism.

H mechanized farming.

J mining.

Name ______________________ Date ______________ Class __________

TEKS 16D

3 In both villages and cities of India, residential areas tend to be sorted by

A occupation.

B age.

C *jati*, or caste.

D haphazardly.

Check your answers.
If you missed 0, great job!
If you missed 1, not bad.
If you missed 2-3, review the comparison of life in urban and rural areas.

Name ______________________ Date ______________ Class ____________

TEKS 17A

Choose the best answer for each question. Circle the letter for the correct answer, or record your answer and fill in the bubbles on the provided griddable.

1 This table shows the religious diversity of India.

Religion	Percentage of Population
Hindu	80.5 %
Muslim	13.4%
Christian	2.3%
Sikh	1.9%
Buddhist	0.8%
Jain	0.4%
Other	0.7%

Source: Census of India

The predominant religion in India is

A Islam.

B Christianity.

C Buddhism.

D Hinduism.

---

2 Central America and the Caribbean cultures are a mix of indigenous with

F Asian, South American, and North American.

G Asian, North American, and European.

H North American, European, and African.

J Asian, European, and African.

Culture

Name ______________________ Date ______________ Class __________

TEKS 17A

3 In Australia, livestock is raised in the dry interior on huge pieces of land called

A ranches.

B mega-farms.

C subsistence farms.

D stations.

Culture

Check your answers.
If you missed 0, great job!
If you missed 1, not bad.
If you missed 2-3, review patterns of culture that make places distinctive.

Name ______________________ Date ______________ Class __________

TEKS 17B

Choose the best answer for each question. Circle the letter for the correct answer, or record your answer and fill in the bubbles on the provided griddable.

Culture

1 In Buddhism, the ultimate goal is to achieve an end to suffering, or

A salvation.

B the Eight-fold Path.

C Nirvana.

D dharma.

---

2 In Hinduism, the form in which a soul is reborn is determined by

F reincarnation.

G karma.

H Vishnu.

J dharma.

Name ______________________ Date ______________ Class __________

TEKS 17B

3 The Quran is the holy book of Muslims. Here is a quotation:

> ***"In the Name of Allah, the Compassionate,***
> ***the Merciful,***
> ***Praise be to Allah, the Lord of the World,***
> ***The Compassionate, the Merciful,***
> ***Master of the Day of Judgment,***
> ***Only You do we worship, and only You***
> ***Do we implore for help.***
> ***Lead us to the right path,***
> ***The path of those you have favored***
> ***Not those who have incurred***
> ***Your wrath or***
> ***Have gone astray."***
>
> **—The Quran**

"Allah" refers to

A Muhammad.

B Mecca (Makkah).

C God.

D Shiite Muslims.

Check your answers.
If you missed 0, great job!
If you missed 1, not bad.
If you missed 2-3, review major world religions.

Name ______________________ Date ______________ Class ________

TEKS 17C

Choose the best answer for each question. Circle the letter for the correct answer, or record your answer and fill in the bubbles on the provided griddable.

1 The first country in the world to allow full woman suffrage was

A New Zealand.

B the United States.

C Russia.

D Switzerland.

---

2 Women have become heads of state in the Northwestern European countries of

F Germany, United Kingdom, and Norway.

G France, Spain, and Italy.

H Sweden, Finland, and United Kingdom.

J Switzerland, Austria, and Germany.

Culture

Name ______________________ Date ______________ Class __________

TEKS 17C

3 In the countries of the Arabian Peninsula, married women are expected to

A work outside the home to contribute to family income.

B keep house, raise the children, and make a comfortable home for their husbands.

C participate in the community's political life.

D attend college.

Culture

Check your answers.
If you missed 0, great job!
If you missed 1, not bad.
If you missed 2-3, review opportunities for women, ethnic minorities, and other underrepresented groups.

Name ______________________ Date ______________ Class __________

TEKS 17D

Choose the best answer for each question. Circle the letter for the correct answer, or record your answer and fill in the bubbles on the provided griddable.

1 Texas's cowboy tradition represents contributions from the cultures of

A Europeans, Anglo Americans, and Spanish.

B Native Americans, Anglo Americans, and Spanish.

C Spanish, Europeans, and Asians.

D Asians, Native Americans, and Spanish.

---

2 From the 1980s, most immigrants to New Zealand have come from

F the Pacific Islands, Asia, Africa, and the Middle East.

G North America, South America, and Asia.

H Asia, the Pacific Islands, and North America.

J Africa, South America, and Europe.

Name ______________________ Date ______________ Class ________

TEKS 17D

3 South Africa's official languages include English, Afrikaans, and how many African languages?

A none

B one

C five

D nine

Culture

Check your answers.
If you missed 0, great job!
If you missed 1, not bad.
If you missed 2-3, review the contributions of diverse groups to multicultural societies.

Name ______________________ Date ______________ Class __________

TEKS 18A

Choose the best answer for each question. Circle the letter for the correct answer, or record your answer and fill in the bubbles on the provided griddable.

1 From the early 1990s, the former Yugoslavia broke up into independent countries based on ethnic groups.

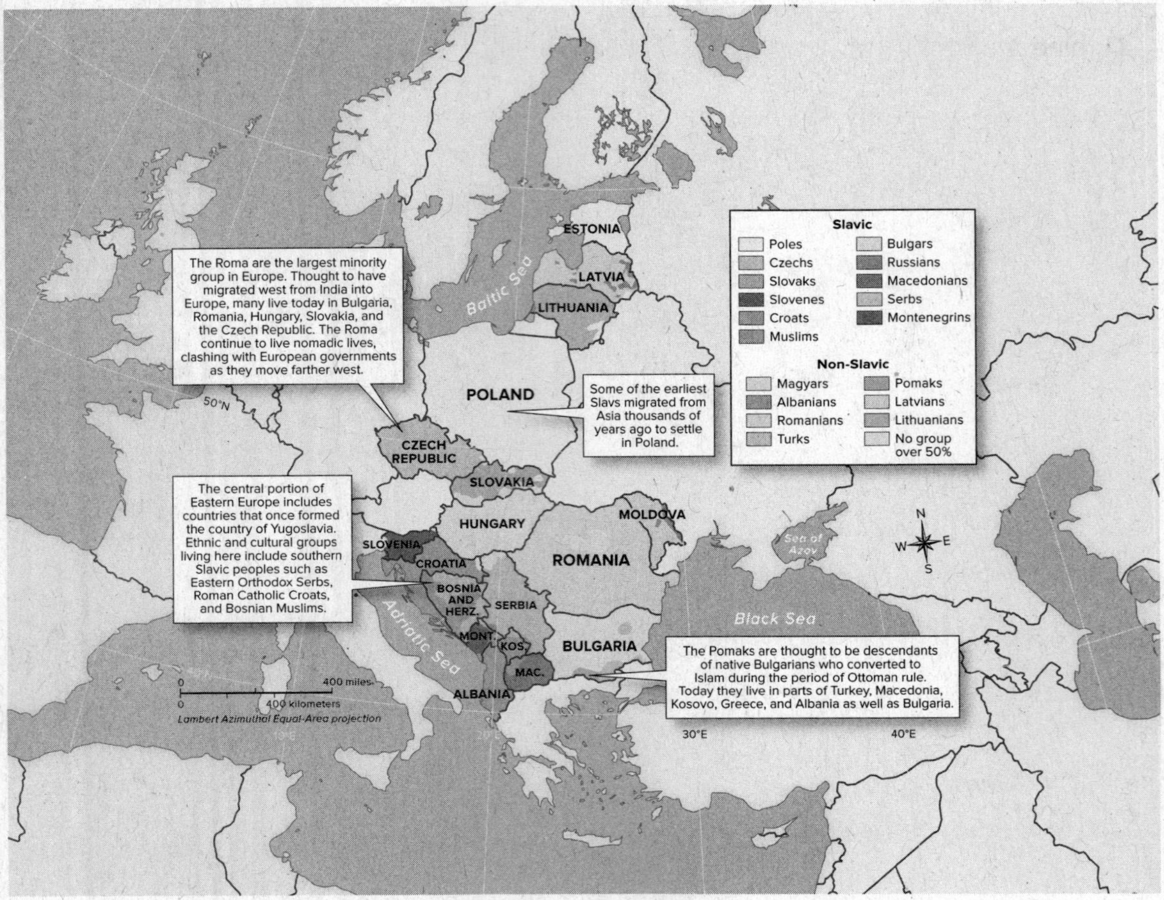

Which of the countries has the greatest ethnic mix?

A Slovenia

B Croatia

C Bosnia and Herzogovina

D Serbia

Name ______________________ Date ______________ Class ________

TEKS 18A

2 As a result of European colonial rule and settlement, most people in Southern Africa today follow the religion of

F animism.

G Islam.

H Hinduism.

J Christianity.

---

3 The transportation innovation that tied the Pacific Coast of Russia to the economic and political heart of the country was

A a major highway.

B the Trans-Siberian Railway.

C airlines.

D ships.

Culture

Check your answers.
If you missed 0, great job!
If you missed 1, not bad.
If you missed 2-3, review cultural changes in specific regions caused by migration, war, trade, innovations, and diffusion.

TEKS 18B

Culture

Choose the best answer for each question. Circle the letter for the correct answer, or record your answer and fill in the bubbles on the provided griddable.

1 In 1994 a violent genocide erupted in Rwanda over

A the favored position of the minority Tutsi people.

B the favored position of the Hutu.

C land disputes.

D religious disputes.

---

2 The Muslim fundamentalist Taliban allowed al-Qaeda and its leader Osama bin-Laden to live in

F Georgia.

G Azerbaijan.

H Afghanistan.

J Pakistan.

Name ____________________ Date ____________ Class ________

TEKS 18B

3 After the breakup of Yugoslavia, ethnic groups in Bosnia-Herzogovina, especially Bosnian Croats and Bosnian Muslims, were attacked by

A Slovenians.

B al-Qaeda.

C Serbs.

D Russians.

Culture

Check your answers.
If you missed 0, great job!
If you missed 1, not bad.
If you missed 2-3, review causes and perceptions of conflicts between peoples.

Name ______________________ Date ______________ Class __________

TEKS 18C

Choose the best answer for each question. Circle the letter for the correct answer, or record your answer and fill in the bubbles on the provided griddable.

1 An indigenous group in Equatorial Africa that has maintained its traditional way of life is

A the Mbuti.

B the Bantu.

C the Zulu.

D the Shona.

2 In Mongolia, a major traditional economic activity is

F mining.

G livestock herding.

H crop farming.

J manufacturing.

Name ______________________ Date ______________ Class __________

TEKS 18C

3 In India, about 70 percent of the population live in villages, where most of them

A grow enough food to feed their families.

B work in high-tech industries.

C produce movies.

D work on plantations.

Culture

Check your answers.
If you missed 0, great job!
If you missed 1, not bad.
If you missed 2-3, review cultures that maintain traditional ways.

Name ______________________ Date ______________ Class __________

TEKS 18D

Choose the best answer for each question. Circle the letter for the correct answer, or record your answer and fill in the bubbles on the provided griddable.

1 American popular culture spreads rapidly throughout the world.

> ***"Still, the music did not come so easily. 'You can't rap in Chinese, it's a tonal language.' 'You can't rap in China, they'll censor you.' . . . all sentiments that kept Chinese hip-hop from taking off with a running start. But hip-hop could not be stopped. . . .***
>
> ***To this day, hip-hop still comes head-to-head with censorship and doubts on the ability to rap in Chinese dialects and creativity. Yet, these obstacles provide listeners with the best form of hip-hop music Chinese youth can offer."***
>
> **—Carla Amurao, "From West to Far East: Rappin' and Rockin' the House,"**
> ***Tavis Smiley: China Week, PBS California*, July 2011**

According to Carla Amurao, the main reason why rap and hip-hop have become popular in China is

A it is very much like traditional Chinese music.

B it subtly expresses opposition to the government and authority.

C Chinese people can understand the words well.

D the government supports it.

---

2 After World War II, United States occupying forces helped Japan establish a government that is

F a dictatorial monarchy.

G a military dictatorship.

H a constitutional monarchy.

J a theocracy.

Culture

TEKS 18D

3 Linguists group languages into language families, which have common roots and similarities.

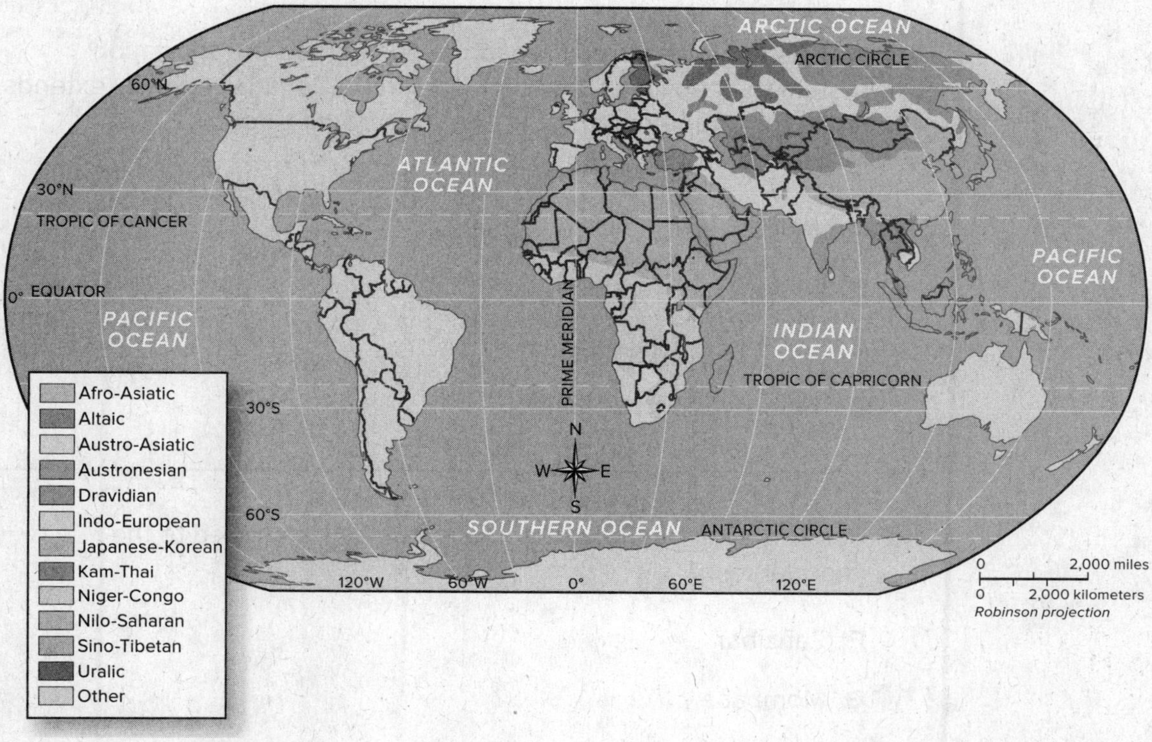

The most widespread language family in the world is

A Indo-European.

B Dravidian.

C Sino-Tibetan.

D Altaic.

Check your answers.
If you missed 0, great job!
If you missed 1, not bad.
If you missed 2-3, review the spread of culture traits.

TEKS 19A

Choose the best answer for each question. Circle the letter for the correct answer, or record your answer and fill in the bubbles on the provided griddable.

1 With its large land area, Canada needs a good transportation system to keep it tied together. The Trans-Canada Highway extends along the southern part of the country from St. John's, Newfoundland, to

A Vancouver, British Columbia.

B Whitehorse, Yukon.

C Edmonton, Alberta.

D Victoria, British Columbia.

---

2 Building a railroad from the coast of Kenya inland led to the importance of

F Zanzibar.

G Mombasa.

H Nairobi.

J Kampala.

TEKS 19A

3 Major cities have grown up in Siberia where

A rivers empty into the Arctic Ocean.

B rivers cross the Trans-Siberian Railway.

C highways intersect.

D pipelines cross the Trans-Siberian Railway.

Check your answers.
If you missed 0, great job!
If you missed 1, not bad.
If you missed 2-3, review the significance of major technological innovations that have been used to modify the environment.

Name ______________________ Date ______________ Class ________

Science, Technology, and Society

TEKS 19B

Choose the best answer for each question. Circle the letter for the correct answer, or record your answer and fill in the bubbles on the provided griddable.

1 Countries on the Arabian Peninsula, with their substantial energy resources and wealth, have enabled settlement and development by

A learning to drink seawater.

B desalinization.

C conserving groundwater.

D burning coal.

---

2 The attractiveness of the Sunbelt of the United States has been increased by

F a return to farming in the region.

G global warming.

H air conditioning.

J a cooling climate.

Name ______________________ Date ______________ Class __________

Science, Technology, and Society

TEKS 19B

3 Colonial rule and European settlement came late to Equatorial Africa but in the late 1800s and early 1900s were eased by

A airplanes.

B invitations from native peoples.

C control of tropical diseases.

D improved highway maps.

Check your answers.
If you missed 0, great job!
If you missed 1, not bad.
If you missed 2-3, review technological innovations that allowed people to adapt to new places.

TEKS 19C

Choose the best answer for each question. Circle the letter for the correct answer, or record your answer and fill in the bubbles on the provided griddable.

1 The effect of mechanized farming in developed countries, such as the United States, was

A a need for more farm workers.

B migration of surplus farm workers to cities.

C an increased demand for horses.

D a decline in crop production.

---

2 The rise of automobiles and airplanes as means of transportation increased the economic and strategic value of the Middle Eastern resource of

F water.

G petroleum.

H gold.

J wheat.

TEKS 19C

3 The rise of manufacturing in the United States Midwest depended on local supplies of

A gold.

B corn.

C coal.

D water.

Check your answers.
If you missed 0, great job!
If you missed 1, not bad.
If you missed 2-3, review environmental, economic, and social impacts of advances in technology on agriculture and natural resources.

TEKS 20A

Choose the best answer for each question. Circle the letter for the correct answer, or record your answer and fill in the bubbles on the provided griddable.

1 GPS (Global Positioning Systems) depend for their function on a network of

A satellites.

B cell phone towers.

C surveyors.

D cartographers.

---

2 The field of *geomatics* combines

F geography and history.

G geography and astronomy.

H cartography and data management.

J data management and computer science.

TEKS 20A

3 The primary and most important function of a GIS (Geographic Information System) is to

A give directions to a destination.

B store locations.

C link locations with their characteristics, or attributes.

D make maps.

Check your answers.
If you missed 0, great job!
If you missed 1, not bad.
If you missed 2-3, review new information technologies

Name ______________________ Date ______________ Class __________

TEKS 20B

Choose the best answer for each question. Circle the letter for the correct answer, or record your answer and fill in the bubbles on the provided griddable.

1 Trading empires arose in Africa's transition zone from about A.D. 700.

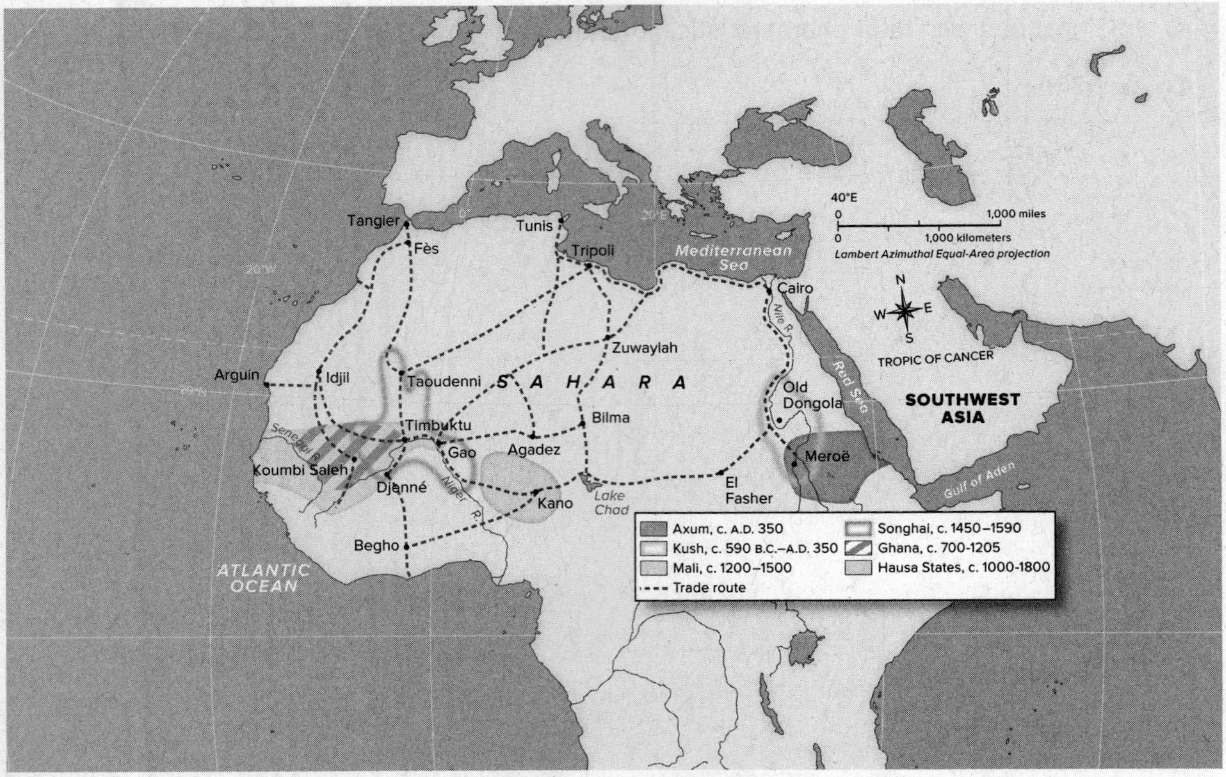

A factor in their decline was

A drought.

B a plant disease.

C European trading posts along the coast, replacing the caravan routes across the desert.

D the rising political power of the United States.

Name ______________________ Date ____________ Class ________

TEKS 20B

2 Increasing the severity of HIV/AIDS in Africa South of the Sahara is

F climate.

G dense vegetation.

H low levels of development with insufficient funds for medical care.

J trade.

---

3 Vancouver, British Columbia, has become an important port in Canada because

A it has beautiful scenery.

B it is a provincial capital.

C it is the closest Canadian port to the growing markets of Asia.

D it is English-speaking.

Check your answers.
If you missed 0, great job!
If you missed 1, not bad.
If you missed 2-3, review effects of technology on societies at different levels of development.

Choose the best answer for each question. Circle the letter for the correct answer, or record your answer and fill in the bubbles on the provided griddable.

1

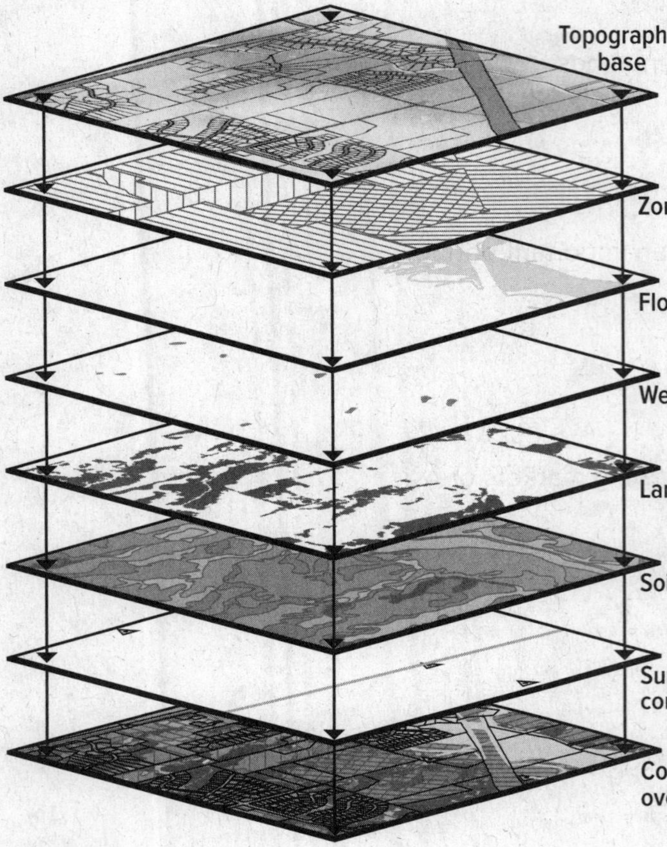

A technology that saves characteristics or attributes of places in layers is a

A map.

B GIS.

C GPS.

D book.

Practice Test

GO ON

2 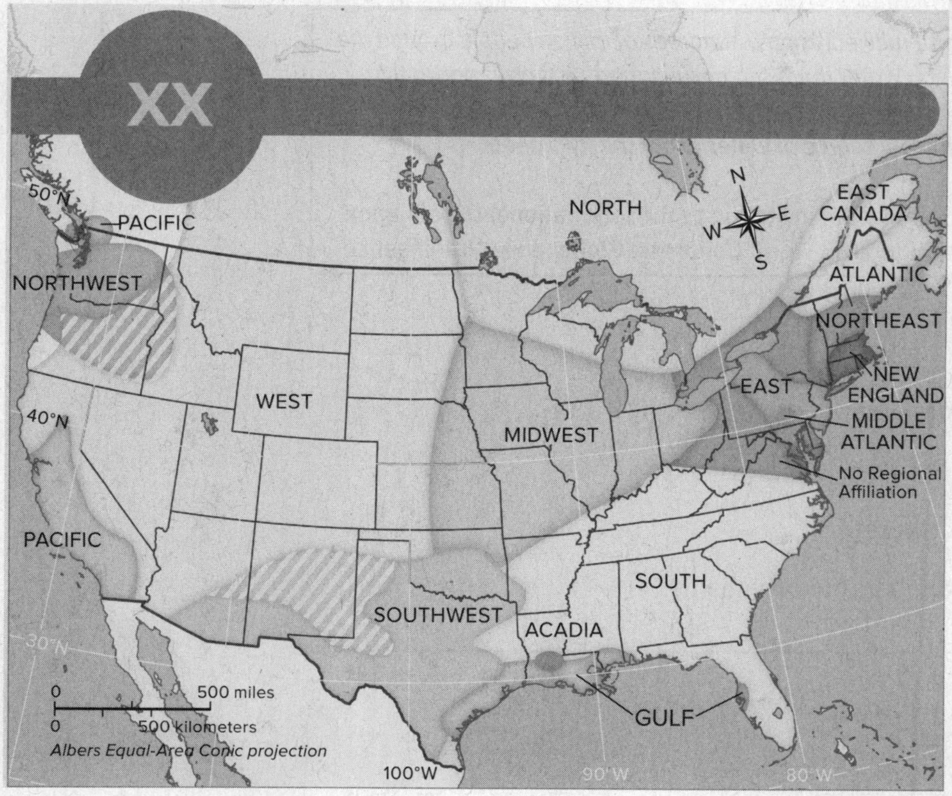

This map shows what kind of regions in the United States and southern Canada?

F formal

G functional

H perceptual

J normal

---

3 According to the theory of plate tectonics, mountains form

A where plates spread apart.

B where plates collide.

C where plates are not moving at all.

D everywhere.

Practice Test

GO ON

4

> *"Desalination is a promise fulfilled. Today, hundreds of million people around the world have access to clean water thanks to desalination. Just as importantly, desalination is also a promise for the future, with its unique ability to deliver a reliable, sustainable and new source of water to our thirsty planet."*
>
> —Corrado Sommariva, invitation to the International Desalination Association 2013 World Congress; Global Water Intelligence

Desalination is

F pumping water from an aquifer.

G digging irrigation canals.

H removing salt from water.

J purifying water from harmful organisms.

5

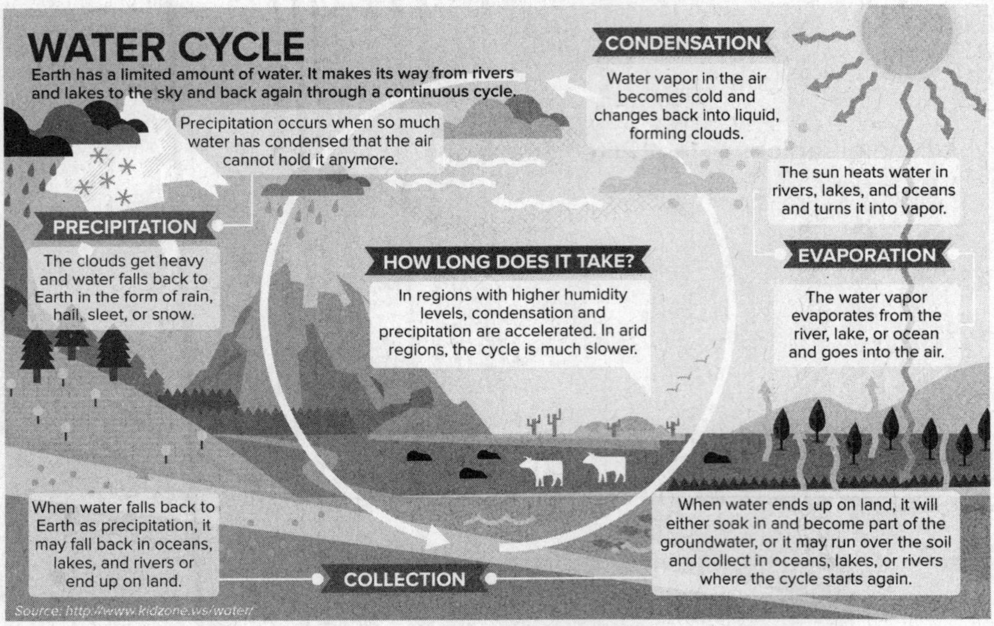

The changing of water from liquid to gas state is

A condensation.

B precipitation.

C conservation.

D evaporation.

GO ON

6 Changes in the summers in Southern Europe are causing

F cooler temperatures and more rain.

G warmer temperatures and less rain.

H warmer temperatures and more rain.

J cooler temperatures and less rain.

---

7 The percentage of water on earth that is freshwater is about

A 50 percent.

B 25 percent.

C 10 percent.

D 3 percent.

---

8 About March 21 and September 23

F the sun's rays strike most directly in the Northern Hemisphere.

G the sun's direct rays strike the Equator.

H the sun's rays strike most directly in the Southern Hemisphere.

J it is the same temperature everywhere on Earth.

GO ON

9

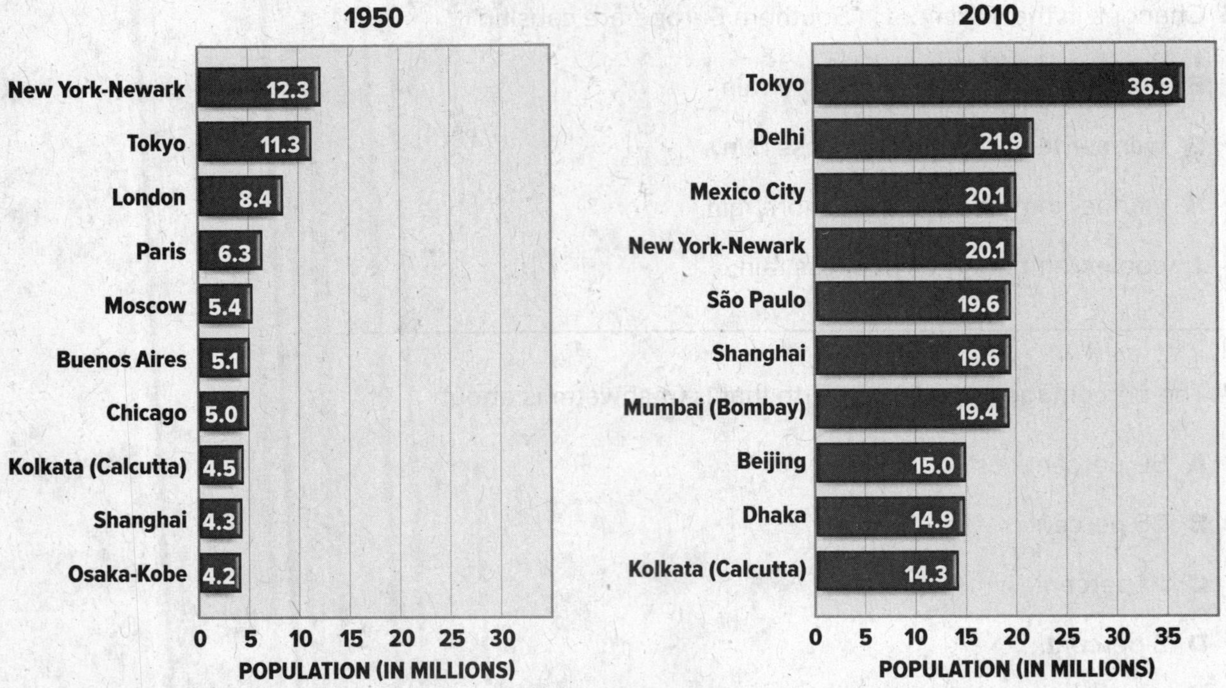

Source: United Nations, Department of Economic and Social Affairs, Population Division, *World Urbanization Prospects: The 2011 Revision*, 2012

Of the ten largest cities in the world in 2010, how many were in the United States?

A 10

B 5

C 3

D 1

GO ON

10

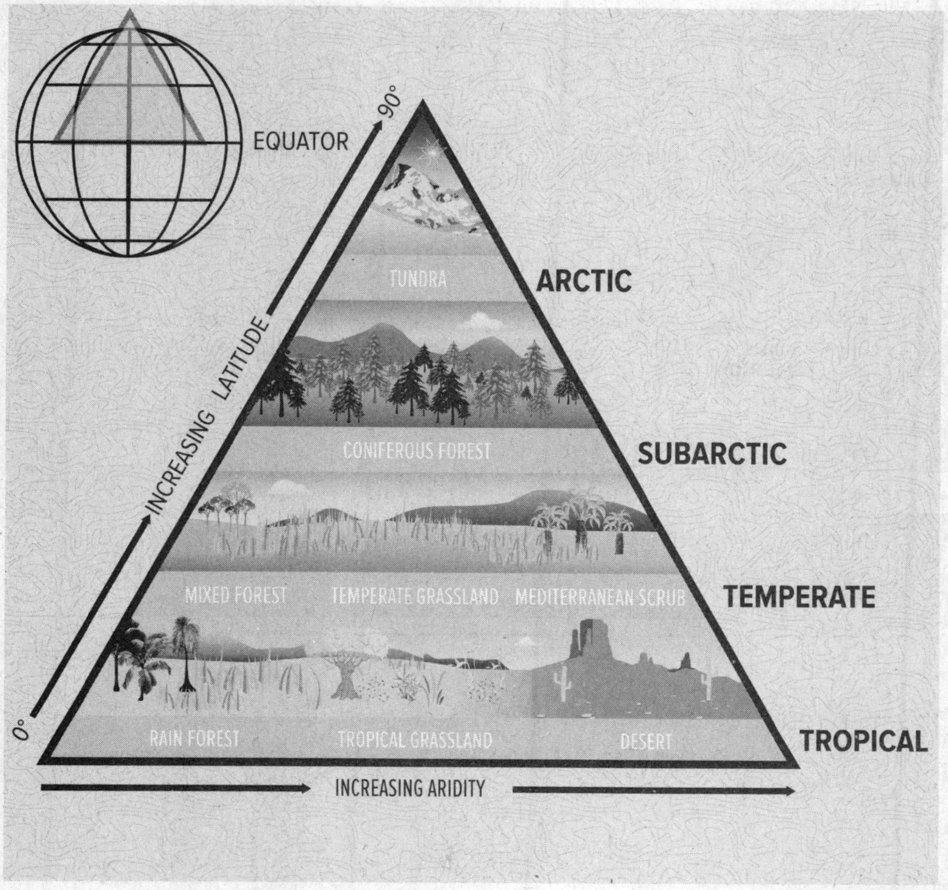

The highest latitude biome that supports trees is

F mid-latitude mixed forest.

G rain forest.

H coniferous forest.

J Mediterranean.

Practice Test

GO ON

11

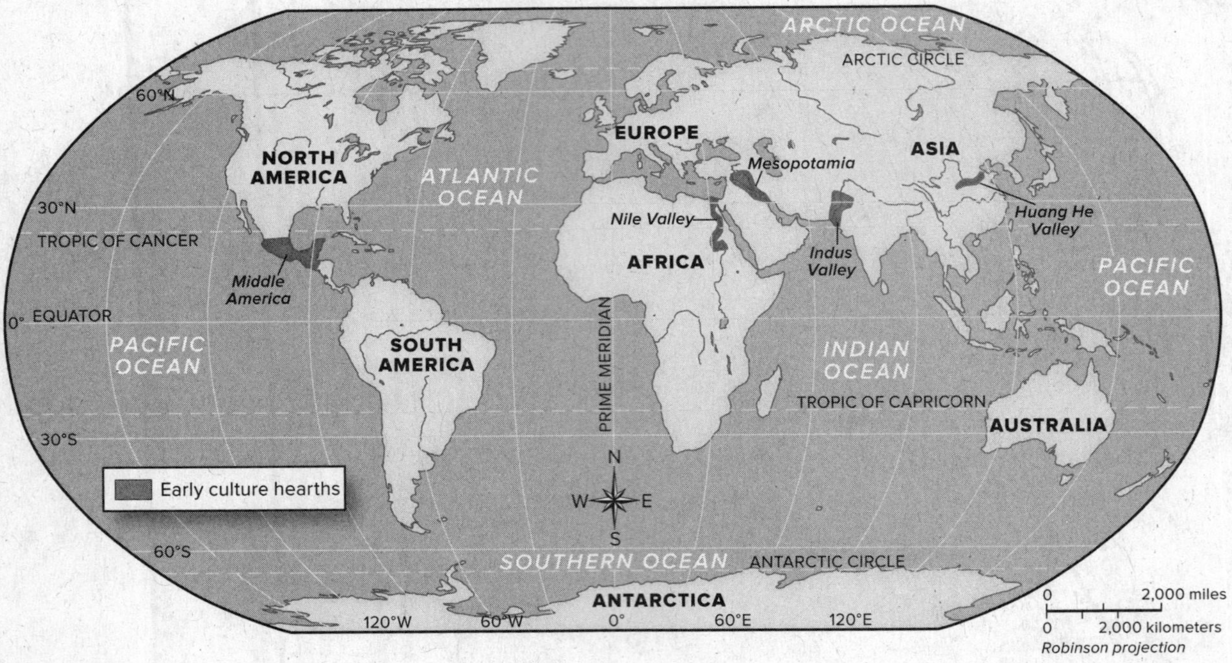

The dark areas on this map represent places where civilization began, or

A cultural diffusion.

B economic systems.

C climate change.

D culture hearths.

---

12 When South Korea embarked on a program of economic development, it focused on

F agriculture.

G mining.

H manufacturing for export.

J highway building.

GO ON

13 A system of government where a small group of people hold all the power is

A a monarchy.

B a constitutional monarchy.

C an oligarchy.

D an autocracy.

14

> ***"In 1961, the [Communist] party predicted . . . that the Soviet Union would have the world's highest living standard by 1980. . . . But when that year came and went, the Soviet Union still limped along, burdened by . . . a stagnant economy."***
>
> —Dusko Doder, "The Bolshevik Revolution," *National Geographic,* October 1992

The failure of the Soviet Union to fulfill the prediction that it would lead the world in living standards by 1980 showed that

F Soviet leadership was incompetent.

G Communist systems lack the incentives that foster business innovation and generation of products that people want.

H the Soviet Union had no resources.

J the Soviet Union lacked a labor force.

---

15 The St. Lawrence Seaway–Great Lakes waterway was instrumental in the economic growth and importance of

A Miami.

B Los Angeles.

C Chicago.

D New Orleans.

GO ON

16

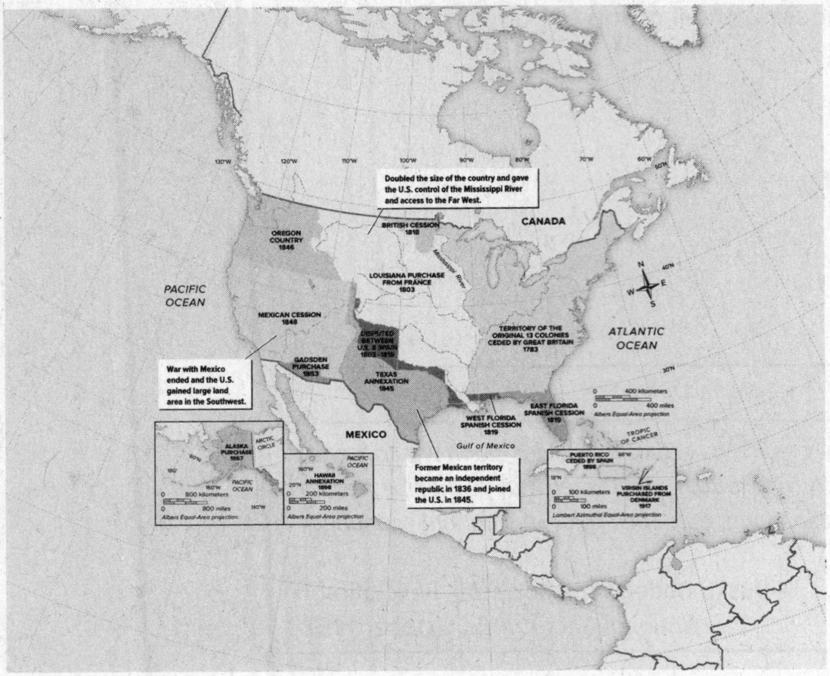

Most of the land that became the state of Texas was acquired by the United States in

F 1803.

G 1819.

H 1848.

J 1845.

---

17 A challenge with the rivers of Siberia is that

A they dry up in summer.

B they frequently change course.

C blocked by ice much of the year, they flood large areas.

D they carry a heavy silt load.

Practice Test

GO ON

18 The base of industrialization in Texas's Gulf Coastal Plain is

F cattle raising.

G cotton raising.

H petroleum and petrochemicals.

J shipbuilding.

19

> ***Sugar maple abundance already has dropped in parts of the northeastern U.S. and southeastern Canada over the past 40 years, primarily because of high acid levels in soils.***
>
> ***The upper Great Lakes region has mostly escaped the damage because its soils are rich in calcium, which provides a buffer against acid. But in an article published this month in the Journal of Applied Ecology, scientists say they've discovered another way that acid rain harms sugar maple seedlings in upper Great Lakes forests.***
>
> ***Donald Zak of the University of Michigan says acid rain prevents dead maple leaves from decaying on the forest floor, creating a barrier that hampers growth of new trees***
>
> **—"Acid Rain Could Kill Maples Near Great Lakes," Associated Press, December 16, 2011**

Acid rain is a danger to young sugar maple seedlings in the Upper Great Lakes because

A it destroys the calcium that acts as a buffer in the soil.

B it causes soil erosion.

C it leads to leaf mold.

D it prevents dead maple leaves from decaying on the forest floor.

GO ON

20 Canada has two official languages, English and

F French.

G Spanish.

H Inuktitut.

J Cree.

21

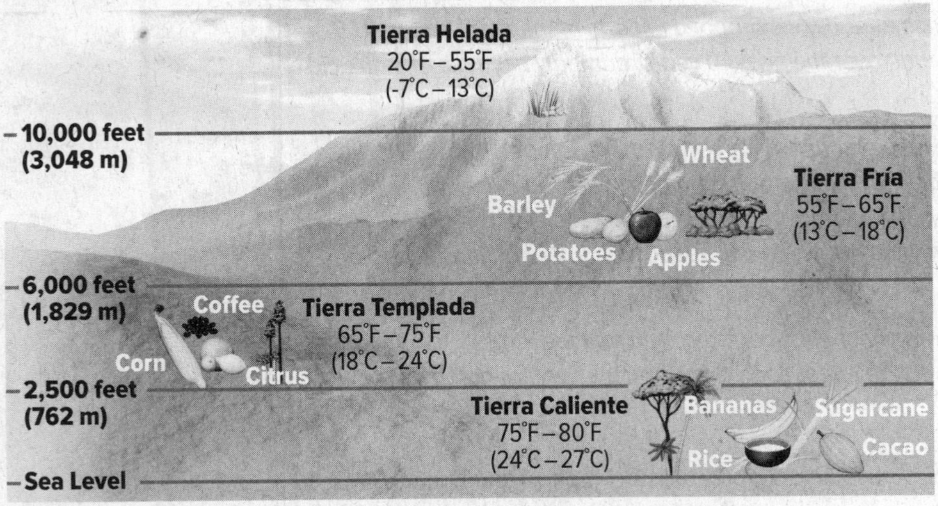

At what elevation are coffee, corn, and citrus grown?

A Sea level to 2,000 feet (762 m)

B 2,500 feet to 6,000 feet (762 to 1829 m)

C 6,000 to 10,000 feet (1829 to 3048 m)

D above 10,000 feet (3048 m)

Practice Test

GO ON

22

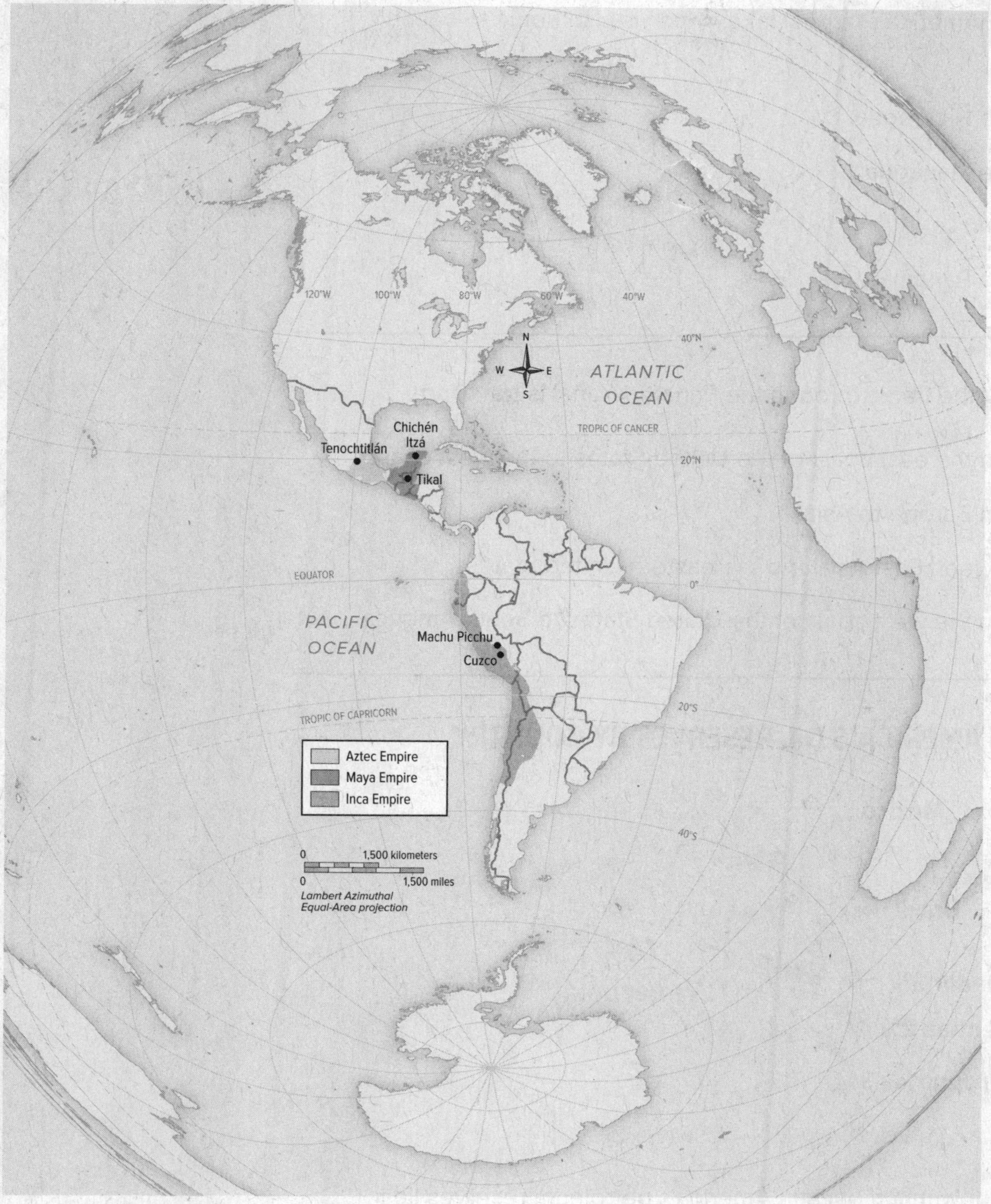

The civilization that flourished in the Yucatán Peninsula was the

F Aztec.

G Maya.

H Olmec.

J Mestizo.

GO ON

23 Central America's largest lake, which is also home to oceanic life, is

A Lake Nicaragua.

B Lake Managua.

C Gatún Lake.

D Lake Panama.

---

24 Most of the traffic through the Panama Canal is traveling

F from the east coast of the United States to the west coast.

G from Europe to Asia.

H between East Asia and the eastern United States.

J from the west coast of the United States to South America.

---

25 **LATIN AMERICA'S OIL RESERVES BY COUNTRY**

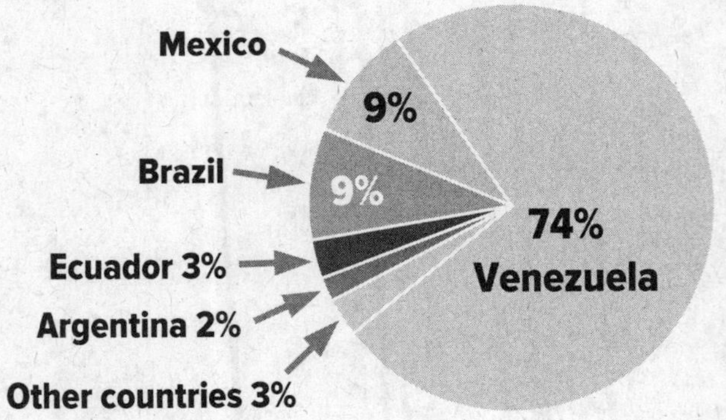

Source: *BP Statistical Review of World Energy, June 2009.*

About how much of Latin America's petroleum reserves lie in Venezuela?

A all

B three-quarters

C one half

D one quarter

Practice Test

GO ON

26 Which of the following was not a contributing factor to political instability in post-independence South America?

F a lack of any tradition of self-government

G control of power by a small elite

H an invasion by the United States

J the rise of powerful caudillos

---

27 The black triangle is a heavily industrialized area that includes

A Poland, Czech Republic, and eastern Germany.

B Eastern Germany, Belarus, and Slovenia.

C Czech Republic, Hungary, and Romania.

D Romania, Hungary, and Croatia.

---

28 The Baltic Sea is unique among the world's water bodies in that

F it is located in the world's coldest region.

G it is a tropical sea.

H its connection with the open ocean is limited, so it is less salty than other seas.

J no rivers empty into it.

---

29 Of the countries of West Africa, the largest in population is

A Mali.

B Côte d'Ivoire.

C Nigeria.

D Ghana.

Practice Test

GO ON

30

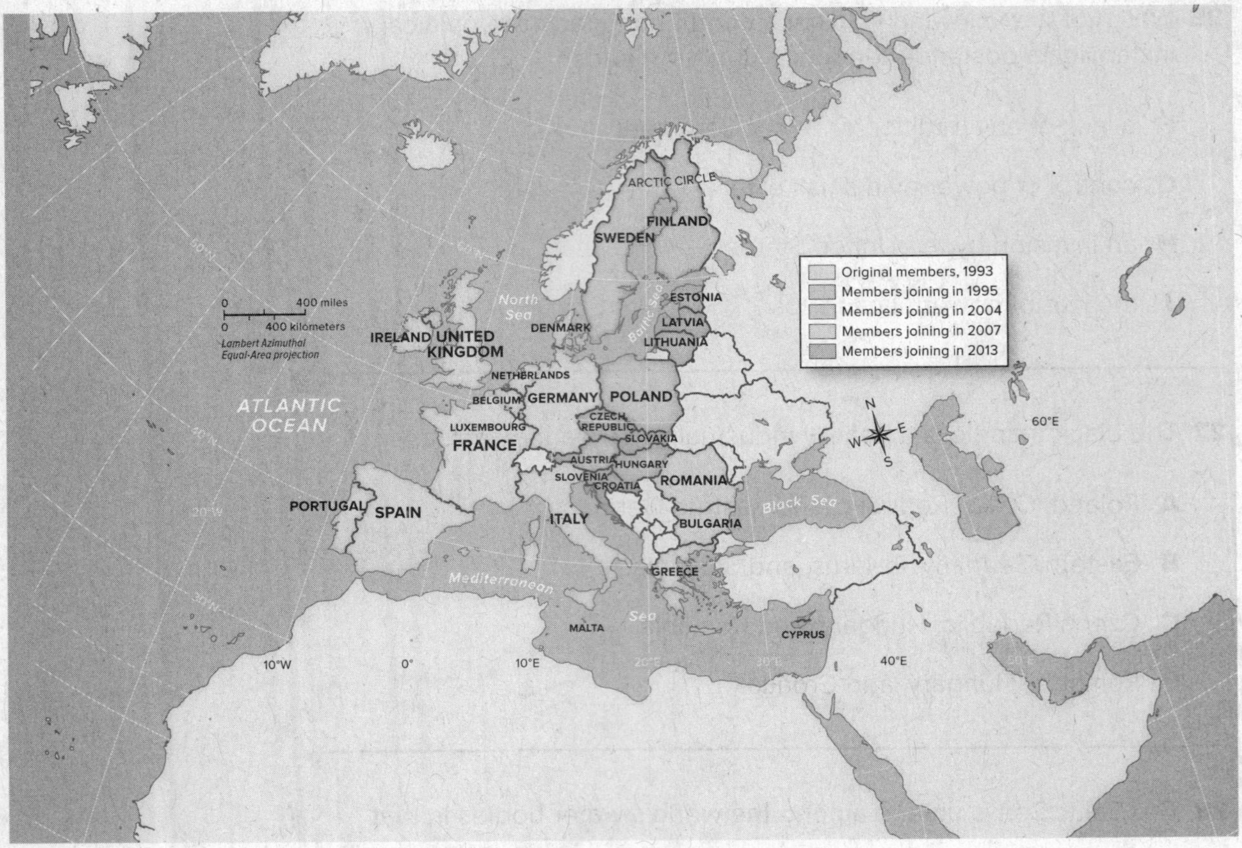

The last country to join the European Union was

F Romania.

G Sweden.

H Switzerland.

J Croatia.

---

31 Which of the following is not an economic problem in Southern Europe that is straining the European Union?

A too much government spending

B high unemployment

C high national debt

D authoritarian governments

Practice Test

GO ON

32 A *shatter belt* is a region that

F has a fragile economy.

G has experienced repeated splintering and fracturing along cultural and ethnic lines.

H has many earthquakes.

J has fragile ecosystems.

33

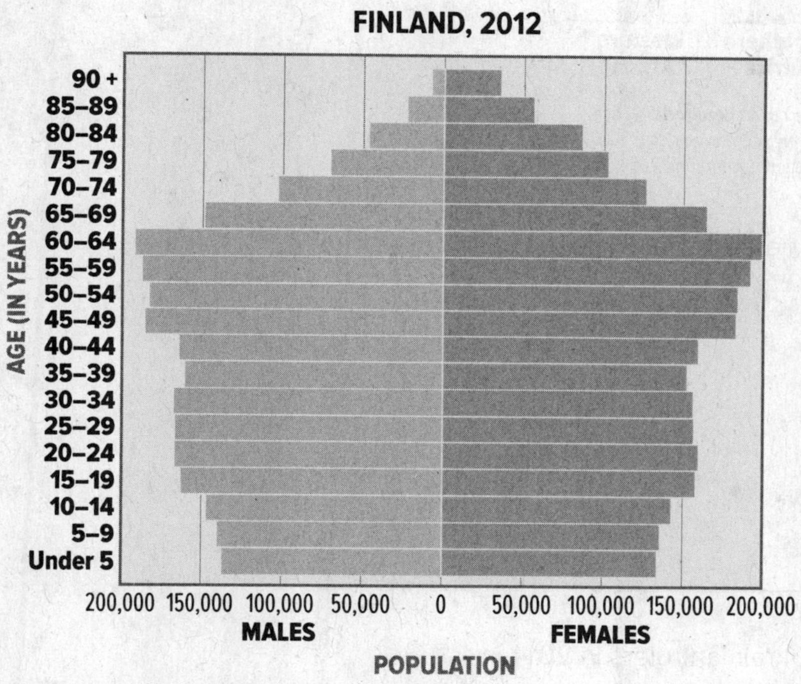

Source: U.S. Census Bureau, International Programs, International Database: 2012

This population pyramid shows that

A Finland's population is aging as people live longer and fewer babies are born.

B Finland's population is growing rapidly as many babies are born, but few survive to old age.

C Finland has large numbers of young-adult immigrants.

D All age groups in Finland are the same size.

Practice Test

GO ON

34

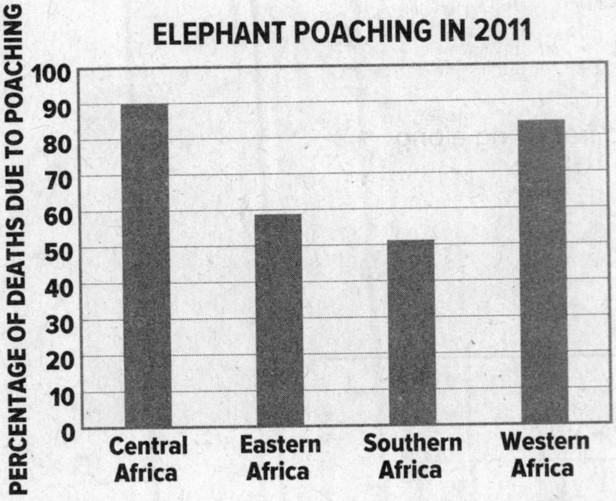

NOTE: Central Africa is sometimes referred to as Equatorial Africa.
Sources: http://www.cntraveler.com/2010; http://ngm.nationalgeographic.com/2012

The region where the largest percentage of elephant deaths is due to poaching is

F Central Africa.

G Eastern Africa.

H Southern Africa.

J Western Africa.

---

35 Pro-Russian rulers replaced Ukrainian rulers in 2014 in

A Chernobyl.

B Kiev.

C Crimea.

D Odessa.

GO ON

36 The reason for the relatively mild climate of Northwestern Europe is

F the latitude.

G a high range of mountains to the north, blocking cold winds.

H a high range of mountains to the west.

J the North Atlantic Current in the nearby ocean and seas.

---

37 Which of the following was not a benefit of the construction of the Aswān High Dam and other dams on the Nile River?

A lack of silt deposit on the banks of the river and the need for more artificial fertilizer

B reduced flooding

C year-round irrigation

D hydroelectric power generation

---

38 An important belief common to Judaism, Christianity, and Islam is

F monotheism.

G observing the seventh day of the week as the Sabbath.

H Jesus as the Son of God.

J fasting during the holy month of Ramadan.

---

39 According to a United Nations report, Israel is the world leader in water recycling. The recycled water is used for

A household use.

B manufacturing.

C agriculture.

D water parks.

Practice Test

GO ON

40

> *"Among all oil exporters, Iraq in 20 years' time will vault past Russia from third to second place, behind only Saudi Arabia, says IEA. The agency expects Iraq single-handedly to provide 45 percent of global production growth between now and 2035.*
>
> *Iraq is 'very, very rich' in energy assets, said Fatih Birol, IEA chief economist and the report's main author. Iraq benefits from having some of the lowest production costs in the world and 'easy geography'."*
>
> —Thomas K. Grose, "Iraq Poised to Lead World Oil Supply Growth, but Obstacles Loom," *National Geographic Daily News*, October 9, 2012

The country that will take second place in oil production (after Saudi Arabia) and account for nearly one half of all growth by 2035 is

F Iran.

G Iraq.

H Libya.

J Kuwait.

---

41 A revolution in 1979 brought to power in Iran a government that is

A a monarchy.

B an oligarchy.

C a theocracy.

D a parliamentary democracy.

---

42 The majority of governments of countries in the Arabian Peninsula today are

F republics.

G parliamentary democracies.

H monarchies.

J theocracies.

GO ON

43 The Great Man-Made River in Libya

A brings water to Libya from the Nile River in Egypt.

B is a series of desalinization plants.

C taps underground aquifers that formed in ancient times when the climate was wetter.

D brings water from Africa South of the Sahara.

---

44 The Silk Road, a trade route through Central Asia, connected

F Moscow and India.

G the Mediterranean basin and China.

H Afghanistan and Moscow.

J India and China.

Practice Test

GO ON

45

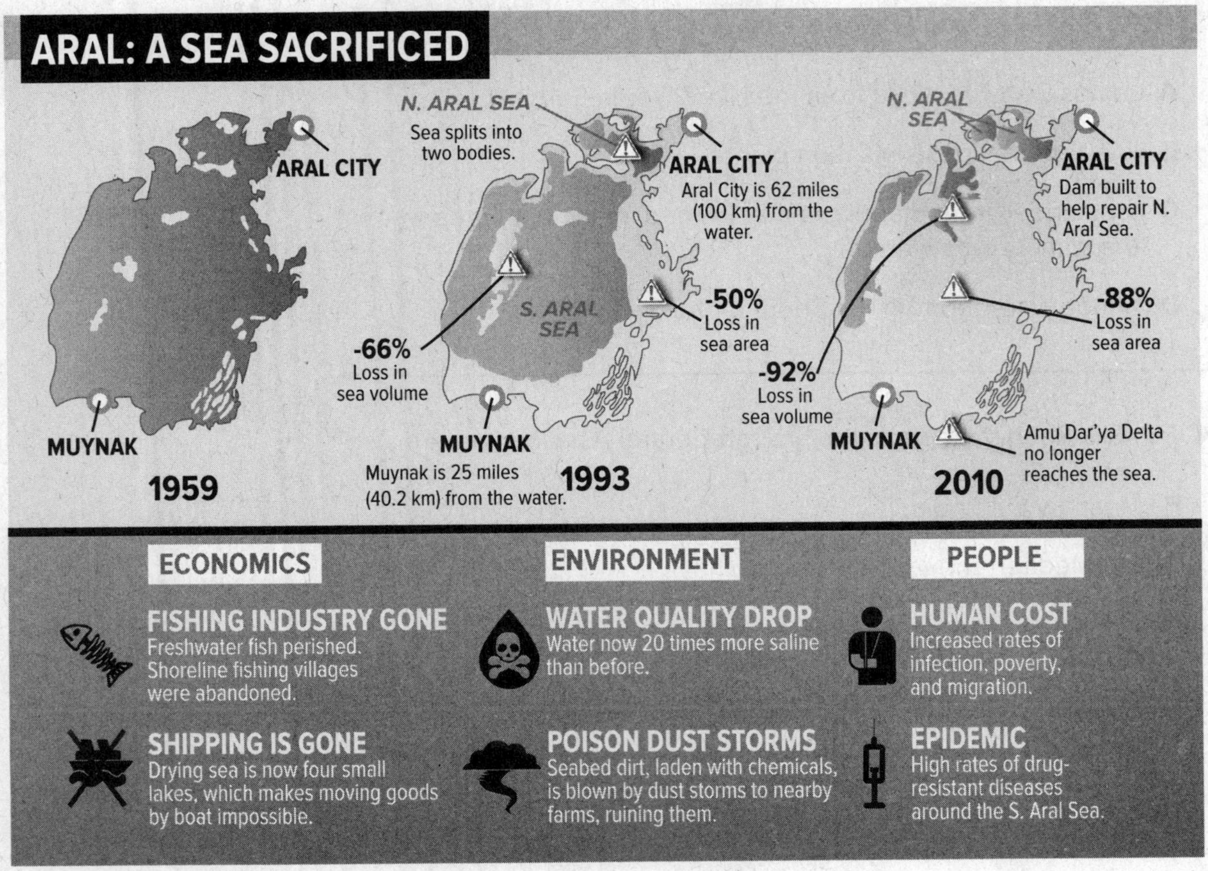

The Aral Sea has suffered from

A global warming.

B invasive species.

C diversion of rivers under Soviet government development schemes.

D a new natural outlet.

---

46 The country with the highest per capita emission of carbon into the atmosphere is

F the United States.

G China.

H India.

J Qatar.

GO ON

47 The most important migration in China today is

A from eastern plains and river valleys to the west.

B from countryside to urban areas.

C from south to north.

D from north to south.

48

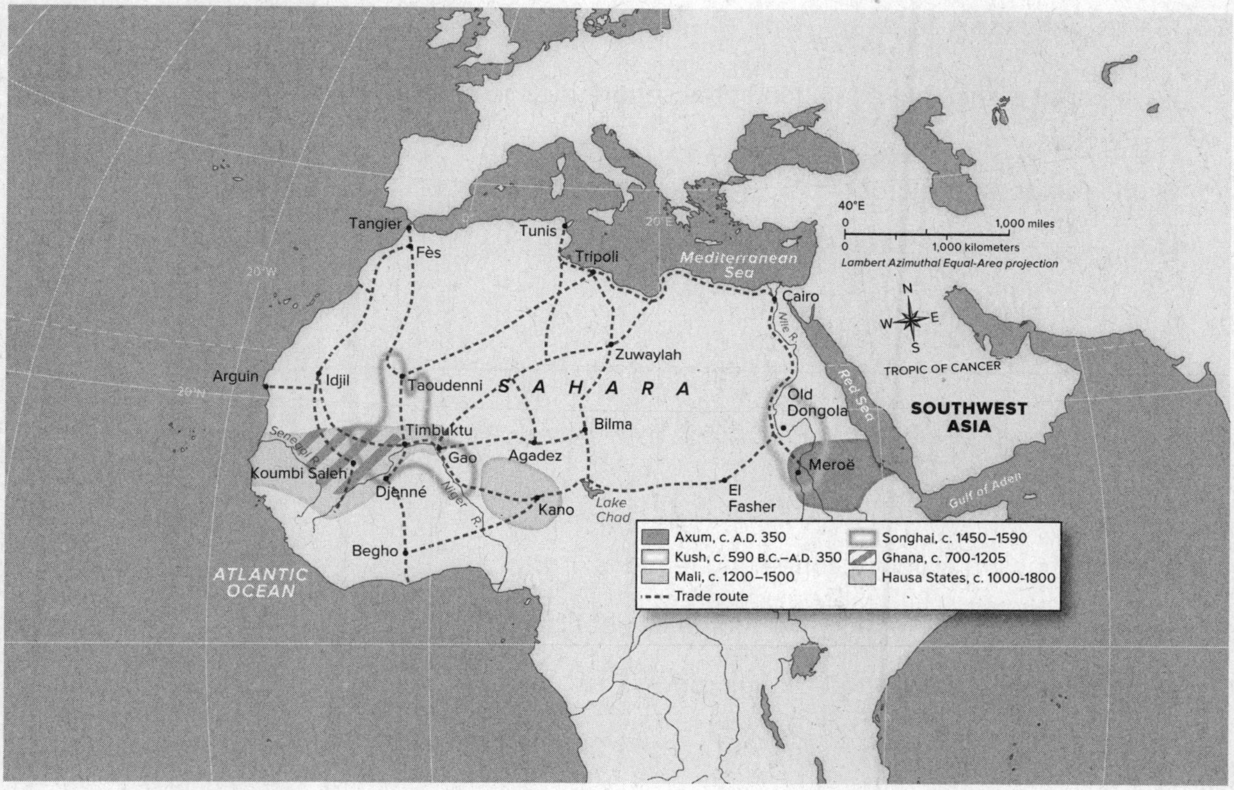

Empires in the western part of Africa's Transition Zone first grew wealthy trading

F camels and cattle.

G tropical hardwoods.

H slaves.

J gold and salt.

Practice Test

GO ON

49 The Rwanda genocide involved

A Europeans killing indigenous peoples.

B Majority Hutus rebelling against favored minority Tutsis.

C Majority Tutsis rebelling against favored minority Hutus.

D An invasion of Rwanda by another African country.

---

50 "Sahel" refers to

F the appearance of vegetation at the southern edge of the Sahara.

G the region where drought is currently affecting the land.

H the southernmost extent of Christianity in West Africa.

J a mountain range.

---

51 European colonial settlers in East Africa established

A small subsistence farms.

B plantations to produce coffee and tea for export.

C large grain farms to grow food for local people.

D no farms—they imported all their food.

Practice Test

GO ON

52

> *"[They] seize upon our subjects, sons of the land and sons of the noblemen, and cause them to be sold; and so great, Sir, is their corruption and licentiousness that our country is being utterly depopulated."*
>
> —Nzinga Mbemba, the king of Kongo, quoted in *East Along the Equator*, 1987

Nzinga Mbemba is describing Portuguese slave traders in Equatorial Africa. Which of the following was not a consequence of this trade?

F an increase in birth rates

G loss of local leadership among African peoples

H loss of food producers among African peoples

J deaths of millions of those seized

---

53 The ancestors of the people of Madagascar came from

A Southeast Asia.

B India.

C the African mainland.

D China.

Practice Test

GO ON

54

Lines of Indian pilgrims walk barefoot through the alleys, drawn by occasional glimpses of the holy river. At last, the alleys fall away, and the sluggish green river appears, smooth as a sheet of glass. From here the view extends to the distant eastern bank, hazed with brown dust. This year, the monsoon rains have been below average, and the Ganges lies low and tame between the banks.

Tens of narrow steps shine wetly. The pilgrims sigh, picking their way down the steps to the water's edge. It's sunrise, the most fortunate hour, and they're here to take a dip in the Ganges.

—Anika Gupta, "The Holy City of Varanasi,"
Smithsonian.com, August 20, 2009

The pilgrims described here are adherents to which major religion?

F Christianity

G Islam

H Hinduism

J Buddhism

---

55 A dispute continues between India and Pakistan about control of

A the Punjab.

B Kerala.

C the Ganges Plain.

D Kashmir.

---

56 An important factor in Botswana's healthy, fast-growing economy is

F foreign ownership of all of the country's mineral resources.

G excellent farmland.

H partnership with DeBeers for sharing the profits of mining diamonds.

J its manufacturing sector.

GO ON

57 Northern Bangladesh has a humid subtropical climate because

A it is located in the low latitudes.

B the Himalaya block cold winds from the north.

C it is subject to monsoons.

D it is subject to earthquakes.

---

58 A threat from climate change for Maldives may be

F drought.

G flooding rains.

H rising sea level.

J mud slides.

---

59 Pakistan and Bangladesh, 1000 miles apart, were once one country. The unifying factor was

A religion.

G language.

C ethnicity.

D physical environment.

---

60 The dominant religion in Nepal is

F Buddhism.

G Hinduism.

H Islam.

J Christianity.

GO ON

61 Which of the following was not a factor in China's isolation from other cultures in ancient times?

A mountains

B deserts

C plateaus

D swamps

---

62 The Fukushima Daiichi Nuclear Power Station in Japan was destroyed in 2011 by

F an earthquake.

G a typhoon.

H human error.

J a tsunami.

---

63 The Meiji Restoration in Japan in 1868

A restored old Shinto shrines.

B brought back Buddhism as the official state religion.

C embarked on the modernization of Japan.

D sent city dwellers back to the farms.

---

64 North Korea is ruled by

F a president.

G a dynasty.

H a king.

J a theocracy.

GO ON

65

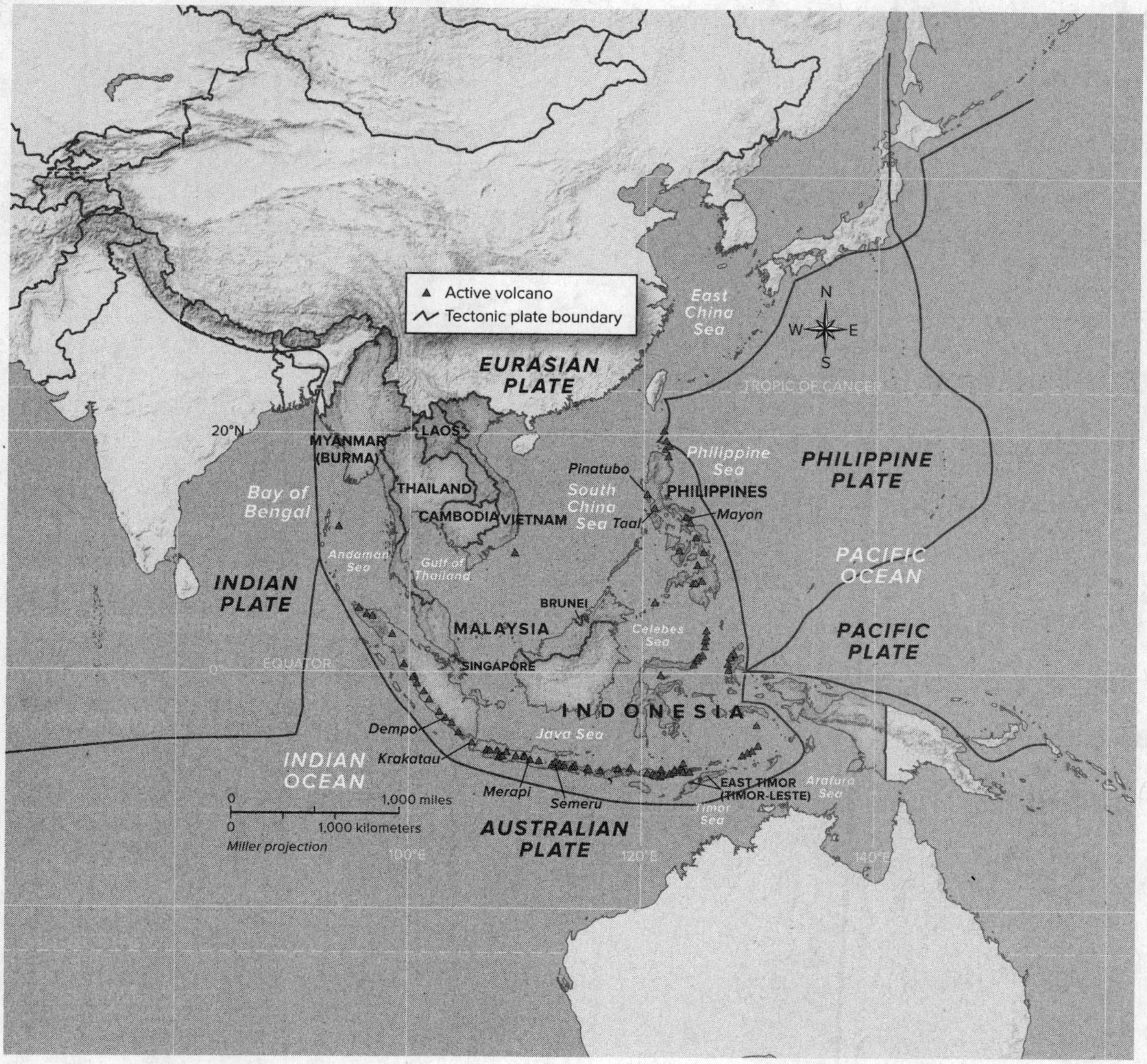

The island of Borneo in Indonesia is unique because it

A is divided between two countries.

B is mountainous.

C has a dry climate.

D has no active volcanoes and rarely experiences earthquakes.

Practice Test

GO ON

66 The largest minority ethnic group in Southeast Asia is

F Chinese.

G Indian.

H Malay.

J European.

---

67 The first European settlement of Australia, in 1788, was

A free settlers seeking gold.

B religious dissidents.

C prisoners.

D whale hunters.

---

68 Atolls form around

F volcanoes in water.

G mountains on land.

H barrier reefs.

J artificial islands.

STOP